The Rise of Virtual Communities

A Simple Guide to Big Ideas

Nova Martian

Contents

Chapter 1

What Are Virtual Communities?

This chapter lays the groundwork for understanding how communities have been transformed by digital technologies. We begin by defining what a community means online—distinguishing it from a mere network—and survey the communication modes and shared digital spaces that make it possible. Next, we trace the emergence of virtual gatherings from early text-based networks to graphical interfaces and the World Wide Web. We then classify the major forms these communities take and examine their core features. Finally, we contrast them with traditional, face-to-face groups and explore what it means to join, participate in, and belong to a community in the digital age.

1.1   Understanding Community in the Digital Age

Sociologists have long grappled with defining what makes a community. At its core, a community is more than just a collection of individuals; it is a social constellation marked by shared identity, a system of norms, and reciprocal relationships. Unlike a mere crowd, members of a community recognize a sense of belonging rooted in overlapping values

1

or experiences. This shared identity allows people to navigate expectations and behaviors, creating a stable framework for social interaction. Reciprocity, meanwhile, ensures relationships are not one-sided but built on mutual exchange—whether of support, information, or trust. Classic examples range from small rural villages to ethnic enclaves, where dense social bonds knit individuals into cohesive wholes.

With the advent of the internet and digital platforms, the very foundations of community have undergone profound transformation. Traditional modes of gathering—physical proximity, habitual meeting places, face-to-face interaction—have expanded to encompass virtual forums, social media, and real-time messaging. These digital tools dismantle geographic constraints that once limited the scope of community life, enabling people separated by continents and cultures to forge meaningful connections. Interaction that was previously bounded by time and location now flows asynchronously and ubiquitously. The speed and scale of communication, as well as the variety of modalities available, reshape not only how people relate to one another but also the expectations around social norms and participation.

It is crucial to distinguish community from the interconnected yet distinct phenomena of networks and audiences in the online realm. A community is characterized by cohesion, shared identity, and norms that bind members into a collective. In contrast, a network is often a more fluid and expansive system of connections, lacking necessarily a shared identity or mutual obligations. For example, professional contacts linked on a platform like LinkedIn form a network—they may share interests but do not necessarily identify as a community. Similarly, an audience is composed of passive recipients of content or communication, without the interactive, reciprocal relationships that define community life. An online forum devoted to a hobby illustrates community through active conversations, mutual support, and emergent norms, while a popular blog gains an audience without cultivating a communal structure.

The digital milieu offers a variety of communication channels, each with its own social affordances—the possibilities they enable or constrain. Text remains foundational, from emails and message boards to real-time chat, allowing for thoughtful, recordable exchanges. The rise of audio and video communication has introduced richer, more immediate and nuanced expressions of human presence. Video calls and livestreams, for example, replicate aspects of physical co-presence, capturing tone, facial expressions, and gestures, enhancing empathy and trust. Each mode shapes how participants engage: text allows reflection and editing, audio conveys emotion and spontaneity, video demands more attentiveness but can create stronger social bonds.

Beyond communication formats, digital communities inhabit shared virtual spaces—online meeting places where interaction unfolds and collective identity is enacted. These range from discussion forums and chat rooms to social media feeds and multiplayer game environments. Such spaces serve as the new "village squares," hosting conversations, rituals, and exchanges of knowledge. Importantly, unlike physical venues bound by walls and hours, digital spaces are persistent and scalable. They archive interactions so newcomers can enter dialogues midstream, titles and roles evolve based on contribution rather than tenure alone, and norms are negotiated anew as communities grow or

3

fragment.

This scalability is a defining feature: online communities can expand from a handful of members to millions while preserving meaningful interaction. Whereas in traditional communities, size often dilutes intimacy and shared governance structures, digital architecture incorporates tools—like subgroups, moderators, and tagging systems—to maintain coherence. Platforms such as Reddit or Facebook host large, diverse communities subdivided into focused sub-communities, enabling people to find their niche while remaining part of a broader collective. The technical capacity for scalability transforms how we conceive community boundaries, raising questions about inclusion, identity, and control that were less pronounced in smaller-scale traditional communities.

Another transformative aspect is the persistence and asynchrony of online communication. Unlike ephemeral face-to-face exchanges, digital conversations remain recorded and searchable, allowing members to engage at their convenience. This removes many temporal barriers, promoting inclusivity for those with differing schedules, abilities, or time zones. Asynchronous interaction also encourages more reflective and nuanced dialogue, as participants can pause, research, and craft responses rather than react immediately. Yet this persistence also amplifies the stakes—comments live on indefinitely, shaping reputations and group memory. The archive of discourse becomes a resource but also a challenge for community management and identity preservation.

The digital age erases geographic limitations that historically constrained community formation. People can transcend local boundaries to unite around shared interests, beliefs, or experiences irrespective of physical location. This global reach fosters transnational communities, such as diasporic groups maintaining cultural ties, global fandoms connecting across continents, or activist networks coordinating international campaigns. These communities navigate cultural differences and linguistic divides through translation tools, hybrid norms, and flexible identities. The expansive reach enriches opportunities for solidarity but complicates governance and norm enforcement due to varied legal and ethical frameworks.

However, these transformations bring distinct challenges. Information overload can overwhelm members, making it difficult to discern meaningful engagement from noise. Moderation becomes a herculean task, as community managers balance openness with the enforcement of norms and the suppression of harmful behaviors. Coordination complexity spikes as communities negotiate diverse member expectations and logistical hurdles inherent to digital platforms. Fragmentation, misinformation, and echo chambers reveal the potential dark sides of digitally mediated community, demanding thoughtful design and active stewardship.

Overall, the digital age reshapes community formation by expanding scale, dissolving geographic anchors, and reconfiguring modes of interaction. While the fundamental sociological pillars of shared identity, norms, and reciprocity remain intact, the settings and tools that sustain these pillars have evolved dramatically. Online communities offer new possibilities for connection and belonging, alongside novel challenges that test our understanding of sociality itself. In this dynamic landscape, community is neither diminished nor simple; it is reimagined—complex, multifaceted, and continuously negotiated in spaces both virtual and real.

1.2 Origins of Virtual Communities

The emergence of virtual communities did not occur overnight but grew steadily from a series of experiments in communication technology and social interaction that predate the familiar chat rooms and social networks of today. To understand how billions now connect online, it helps to trace the roots back to the earliest networked social spaces, where users first discovered the potential of digital gathering. These precursors—bulletin boards, mailing lists, text-based games, and academic networks—laid the foundation not only for today's platforms but for enduring principles of online community life.

The late 1970s and early 1980s witnessed the rise of Bulletin Board Systems (BBSs), which can be thought of as the great-grandparents of modern forums and social media. BBSs were dial-up networks hosted on personal computers, accessible locally or via long-distance phone calls. They attracted hobbyists who shared files, posted messages, and arranged meetups around shared interests—music, technology, or niche hobbies. While initially geographically limited, BBS networks soon began to connect with one another, creating a patchwork of localized enthusiast communities that mirrored the social fabric of small towns. Unlike today's platforms, where billions can meet instantly, BBS users often experienced slower connections and had to patiently wait their turn on limited phone lines, yet they nurtured a vibrant, participatory culture.

Parallel to this, Usenet emerged as a pioneering distributed discussion system born out of academic collaboration. Originating in 1979, Usenet allowed computers to exchange messages in a decentralized fashion, organized hierarchically into newsgroups dedicated to specific topics. Unlike BBSs, which were primarily local, Usenet extended communication across institutions worldwide. This early form of online discussion demonstrated how shared interests could unite otherwise scattered individuals. Meanwhile, ARPANET mailing lists offered another vital channel— email-based forums focused on a particular subject, often academic or technical. These mailing lists evolved into tightly knit affinity groups where expertise and opinions circulated freely, setting precedents for later interest-based online communities.

One of the more imaginative applications of these text-based environments was the creation of Multi-User Dungeons (MUDs) in the late 1970s and early 1980s. Inspired by tabletop role-playing games, MUDs were virtual worlds composed entirely of text descriptions, in which multiple players could interact, solve quests, or simply socialize. MUDs and their object-oriented successors, MOOs (MUD, Object-Oriented), were among the first digital spaces where users crafted collective narratives and identities. Beyond gameplay, they functioned as social experiments—worlds without physical boundaries where participants explored complex interpersonal dynamics, roles, and rules governed largely by the community itself. The MUD experience crystallized the concept that virtual spaces could be more than forums—they could be living, evolving social environments.

At the same time, mailing lists or listservs gained popularity during the 1980s as a powerful tool for organizing around shared passions or professions. More structured than Usenet's sprawling newsgroups, mailing lists

7

facilitated ongoing conversations among members who subscribed via email. Communities formed around everything from science fiction fandom to early software development. The asynchronous nature of these discussions allowed thoughtful exchanges, accountability, and the development of social norms. The distributed yet intimate feeling of listservs made them a precursor to the tightly knit virtual tribes that would later characterize specialized online communities.

University-sponsored networks played a significant role, too, as academic institutions used early computer networks to support collaboration and knowledge-sharing among researchers. These forums were often closed and formal but invaluable for seeding a culture of digital communication. Projects like BITNET and CSNET in the 1980s connected scholars across campuses, establishing not only technical infrastructure but also a social ethos emphasizing openness, peer support, and collective problem solving. The ethos fostered in these communities would ripple outward into the broader public sphere when commercial access became more widespread.

The late 1980s and early 1990s signaled the arrival of proprietary commercial platforms such as AOL, CompuServe, and Prodigy, which ushered in mass-market access to virtual communities. Unlike dial-up BBSs or academic networks that required technical skill or institutional affiliation, these services featured graphical user interfaces and point-and-click navigation designed for ordinary consumers. AOL's chat rooms and message boards became some of the earliest mainstream virtual spaces, welcoming millions who had never before participated in online socializing. These platforms bridged the gap between hobbyists and the general public, introducing many to avatar-driven interaction, instant messaging, and moderated discussion forums. However, the closed, corporate-controlled nature of these services also presaged continuing tensions around governance and user autonomy.

This shift toward graphical interfaces was one of the most transformative milestones. Early online interactions had been largely text-based, often command-line driven, requiring memorization of instructions and patience with slow connections. Graphical user interfaces (GUIs) made communities more accessible, enjoyable, and visually engaging. The introduction of web browsers such as Mosaic in 1993 accelerated this evolution by facilitating hyperlink-driven navigation through the burgeoning World Wide Web. Suddenly, virtual communities could be discovered through web directories and search engines rather than buried in obscure network addresses—dramatically lowering barriers to entry.

Several key platforms epitomize these growing pains and triumphs. The WELL (Whole Earth 'Lectronic Link), launched in 1985, combined ideas from earlier systems into a relatively open forum emphasizing user self-governance and deep, thoughtful conversation. Communities on The WELL demonstrated how digital discussion could foster real social bonds and norms. Later, sites like GeoCities (1994) allowed users to build personal web pages grouped by neighborhood themes, a precursor to the user-generated content and profile-driven spaces of social media. Meanwhile, ICQ and early Instant Messaging services experimented with presence awareness and real-time social interactions, further shrinking the gulf between virtual and physical engagement.

The arrival of the World Wide Web altered online

community dynamics irreversibly. Through hyperlinks, users could navigate from one interest group to another effortlessly, enabling rapid discovery and cross-pollination of ideas. Websites blossomed as hubs for fan clubs, political activism, and professional networking alike. The web's openness created both opportunities and challenges: communities could flourish without gatekeepers, but issues of moderation and identity management became more complex. It was also on the web that new forms of participation emerged—blogs, forums, and eventually platforms supporting multimedia content, laying the groundwork for contemporary social ecosystems.

Despite vast technological changes, early virtual communities imparted fundamental lessons that endure today. Persistence—the archival nature of postings and the ability to return to conversations—affords continuity and collective memory. Self-governance, whether through elected moderators or community norms, helps maintain order and inclusivity. Perhaps most crucially, shared purpose or interest remains the glue that binds members, from hobbyist BBS users to global fandoms. These principles echo through every new platform iteration, revealing a remarkable continuity beneath the surface of ever-changing digital forms.

In tracing the origins of virtual communities, we see an unfolding story of human creativity and social adaptation. What began as modest experiments among technologists and hobbyists has transformed into an integral aspect of modern life, shaping how diverse populations connect across boundaries of geography, culture, and circumstance. Each early innovation contributed layers of insight and infrastructure, building toward the complex, rich social ecosystems we navigate online today.

1.3 Types of Virtual Communities

Understanding the diverse landscape of virtual communities begins with sorting them into recognizable categories. Categorization might seem like an academic exercise, but it is a vital step toward grasping the distinct social dynamics, cultural norms, and technological affordances that define these online gathering places. Much as cities differ from villages in their social fabric and infrastructure, virtual communities vary widely in how they form relationships, share information, and govern interaction. By classifying these digital groups, we gain clearer insights into their roles in users' lives and their impact on society.

One of the earliest and most enduring forms of virtual communities manifests in *discussion forums* or message boards. These platforms operate much like digital town halls or libraries where participants engage in threaded conversations. The hallmark of forums is their structured layout: questions, answers, and debates unfold in clearly demarcated threads that facilitate focused, in-depth dialogue. Originating in the 1980s with bulletin board systems (BBS) and later growing through Usenet newsgroups, discussion forums cater to those seeking detailed knowledge exchange or thoughtful debate. Websites such as Reddit or Stack Exchange exemplify this model, allowing communities to self-organize around specific interests, with moderation and voting systems shaping content quality. These forums often emphasize textual communication and persistency, preserving records of collective wisdom and unresolved disputes alike.

In contrast, *social networking sites* center their community experience on personal profiles and dynamic friendships. Platforms like Facebook and Instagram invite users to construct curated identities, build friendship graphs, and engage through ephemeral news feeds tailored by algorithms. These sites thrive on immediacy and broad social connectivity rather than deep, topic-focused discussions. Here, communication is often casual, multimedia-rich, and emotively charged, with "likes," comments, and shares serving as the currency of social interaction. The architecture of these networks promotes rapid dissemination of personal updates, memes, and cultural moments, weaving a web of social ties that blends the intimate with the performative. More than mere communication tools, social networks have evolved into complex ecosystems where users balance authenticity, visibility, and community belonging.

Meanwhile, the realm of *gaming communities* offers an immersive social experience markedly different from forums and social networks. These communities bundle players into guilds, clans, or factions within massively multiplayer online (MMO) worlds—dynamic environments where collaboration, competition, and role-playing converge. Games like *World of Warcraft*, *Fortnite*, or *Final Fantasy XIV* provide spaces where social bonds are forged in the heat of coordinated quests or competitive battles. Here, identity is shaped not only by text or avatars but also by shared narratives and achievements woven into the virtual world. Governance often emerges organically through leadership roles within guilds or in-game rules maintained by developers. These communities highlight how virtual sociality can mimic, and sometimes transcend, real-world group dynamics through gamified structures and immersive storytelling.

Professional networks occupy a distinct niche, focusing on occupational interests and career development. Platforms such as LinkedIn and specialized remote collaboration hubs facilitate networking, job hunting, mentorship, and skill sharing among peers and experts. These communities prioritize reputation, credentials, and goal-oriented discourse, often featuring groups centered on industries, certifications, or projects. Unlike social networks built around personal life, professional networks impose a degree of formality and trust, with participants aiming to expand influence or knowledge pertinent to their work. Virtual coworking spaces and knowledge-sharing forums complement this ecosystem, enabling remote teams to collaborate asynchronously with structured communication tools. The professional virtual community thus exemplifies how digital spaces can foster economic activity and lifelong learning.

Beyond these broad categories, *interest-based groups* form around shared passions, causes, or specialized knowledge. Whether it is knitting circles on Ravelry, birdwatching enthusiasts on eBird forums, or activists organizing through online petitions, these communities galvanize around mutual enthusiasm and identity. Such groups often operate through smaller, more intimate networks that offer emotional support, practical advice, and collective action. Their boundaries may be porous, allowing members to bridge multiple communities or foster niche subcultures. Unlike the wide reach of social networks, interest-based groups usually cultivate depth over breadth, with rich participatory cultures that celebrate expertise and shared values.

On another front, *content-sharing platforms* create communities centered on the distribution and appreciation of media. Whether through photos on Instagram, videos on YouTube, code repositories on GitHub, or academic papers on ResearchGate, these platforms engineer sociality around the creation and curation of content. Interaction often revolves around commenting, remixing, critiquing, and collaborative creation. The community here is both audience and co-creator, sustained by algorithmic recommendations and tagging systems that connect creators with fans or collaborators. Such spaces are uniquely shaped by the types of media they host, whether ephemeral videos or enduring open-source projects, demonstrating how content format influences social behavior and norms.

More recently, *hybrid communities* have emerged, blending elements of multiple models to create multifaceted ecosystems. Platforms like Discord or Facebook Groups mix forum-like discussion threads, real-time chat, multimedia sharing, and event coordination within a single environment. This melding allows users to fluidly shift between casual chatter, organized knowledge exchange, and collaborative projects without leaving the platform. Such communities reflect evolving user expectations for seamless social experiences, accommodating diverse needs from gaming clans to hobbyist clubs. Hybrid models underscore the intricate layering of social functions now possible online, blurring the lines between previously distinct community types.

Comparing these types across dimensions such as scale, governance, and participation models reveals crucial differences. Forums and interest-based groups often emphasize formal moderation and structured dialogue, promoting sustained focus but sometimes at the cost of accessibility. Social networks scale to billions, relying on algorithmic governance and user-generated norms that evolve rapidly, sometimes unpredictably. Gaming communities balance developer-imposed rules with player-driven hierarchies, fostering cooperative engagement within designed constraints. Professional networks typically enforce verified identities and results-oriented interactions, cultivating trust but limiting spontaneity. Content-sharing platforms vary widely but often depend on reputation systems and community curation to manage quality and participation. Hybrid platforms attempt to synthesize governance strategies from all these areas to maintain coherence while enabling flexibility.

Each community type also differs in participation patterns. Forums encourage thoughtful, asynchronous exchanges; social networks rely on frequent, brief interactions; gaming communities demand synchronized teamwork or competition; professional groups focus on strategic networking and collaboration; content platforms blend passive consumption with active creation; hybrid communities offer layered modes for different engagement levels. Recognizing these patterns helps explain why users gravitate toward certain communities to meet particular social or informational needs.

Amid this diversity, the distinguishing characteristics remain clear. Discussion forums serve as archives of collective inquiry, social networks shape broad identity-play and interpersonal connection, gaming worlds immerse players in shared virtual adventures, professional networks advance career trajectories, interest groups nourish passion-driven bonding, content-sharing platforms enable creative exchange, and hybrid communities unify these functions in versatile hubs. Together, these types illustrate how virtual spaces adapt to human desires for knowledge, belonging, competition, creativity, and collaboration—each forging unique social ecologies in the digital age.

1.4 Key Features and Characteristics

At the heart of every virtual community lies a constellation of features that define its unique existence and shape the social fabric binding its members. Unlike physical communities bound by geography, these digital collectives are distinguished by how they construct identity, enforce norms, allocate roles, govern interactions, communicate, and cultivate culture— all underpinned by technology. Understanding these core elements reveals not only what makes a virtual community thrive but also how it mirrors and transforms human sociality in the digital realm.

- **Identity and Representation**

    Identity in virtual communities is a multifaceted construct shaped primarily through usernames, avatars, and user profiles. Unlike face-to-face interactions where physical appearance and mannerisms convey identity, virtual spaces rely on digital personas—choices made by members to express themselves within the community's cultural framework. A username can be playful, cryptic, or transparent, signaling inclusivity, irony, or expertise. Avatars extend this self-presentation, ranging from simple icons to elaborate digital portraits, sometimes animated or customizable, enabling a form of identity play and experimentation impossible offline.

    Profiles compile these elements alongside additional personal or interest-based information, serving both as a social résumé and an introduction to a member's standing within the community. The fluidity of identity here allows for exploration and reinvention but also raises

16

questions about authenticity and trust. Many virtual communities develop norms around honest self-representation, while others embrace anonymity or pseudonymity as liberating tools for expression. This dynamic tension between visibility and privacy is a defining characteristic, shaping how relationships and reputations form online.

- **Norms and Rules**

  Just as neighborhoods have unwritten codes—for example, returning borrowed tools or keeping noise levels down—virtual communities establish guidelines to maintain order and foster positive interaction. These take the form of explicit community guidelines, terms of service, and codes of conduct that specify acceptable behavior. Beyond formal rules, tacit norms emerge through daily interaction: who speaks when, what topics are taboo, how disagreements should be handled.

  Enforcement varies widely. Some communities empower elected or appointed moderators to police content, issue warnings, or ban transgressors. Others rely on peer pressure, reputation systems, or algorithmic moderation. These dynamics serve several purposes: protecting members from harassment, preventing spam or misinformation, and preserving the tone and focus that attract participants in the first place. The effectiveness and fairness of rule enforcement can profoundly influence a community's health, inclusivity, and longevity.

- **Member Roles**

  Within virtual communities, roles are often more fluid than in traditional societies but remain

17

crucial for structure and functionality. Regular participants create and consume content, engage in discussion, and uphold norms. Yet, distinct positions such as moderators, administrators, and founders carry special responsibilities and powers. Moderators act as on-the-ground caretakers, managing conversations, mediating disputes, and implementing community policies. Administrators oversee these processes and often handle technical aspects or community-wide decisions.

Notably, the boundaries between these roles may blur, with some members cycling through different capacities over time as they gain trust or interest. The distribution of roles often reflects community size, purpose, and governance style. In fan communities, passionate contributors may organically emerge as leaders, whereas corporate-led platforms may impose hierarchies. Each model reflects differing balances between grassroots engagement and institutional control.

- **Governance Structures**

  Governance in virtual communities involves the rules and processes that steer decision-making and conflict resolution. These may be explicitly codified, informal consensus-building mechanisms, or even algorithmically enforced protocols. Some communities resemble microcosms of democratic societies, holding elections for moderators, soliciting member feedback, and maintaining transparent policies. Others adopt top-down governance, issuing unilateral decisions or heavily moderated environments.

  Emerging models blend traditional governance

with new digital possibilities: blockchain-based consensus, reputation-weighted voting, or automated moderation powered by artificial intelligence. Governance not only shapes day-to-day operations but also affects trust, legitimacy, and member empowerment. Disputes over governance often reveal underlying tensions about authority, participation, and the community's evolving identity.

- **Communication Modalities**

  The channels through which members interact form the lifeblood of any virtual community. These modalities fall largely into two categories: synchronous and asynchronous communication. Synchronous channels—such as live chat, voice conferencing, or video calls—simulate real-time conversation, fostering immediacy and spontaneity. They are well-suited to gaming communities, live events, or brainstorming sessions where rapid exchange energizes collaboration.

  Asynchronous communication, typified by forums, email lists, and comment threads, allows members to participate across time zones and schedules. It supports more thoughtful deliberation and enduring conversations, often forming extensive archives of community knowledge. Many communities deploy a hybrid model, leveraging the strengths of each channel to meet diverse needs. The chosen mix profoundly affects participation patterns, inclusivity, and the pace of community evolution.

- **Technological Infrastructure**

  Beneath the visible interactions lies a complex

technological infrastructure that enables and shapes the virtual community experience. Servers host content and manage data traffic, while platform backends coordinate user authentication, message routing, and storage. Application Programming Interfaces (APIs) allow integration with external tools, enabling bots for moderation, content curation, or analytics.

Tools designed for moderation automate detection of spam, offensive language, or rule violations, providing essential support to human moderators. The design and scalability of these technologies influence how communities grow, adapt, and resist disruption. Furthermore, technological affordances—such as limits on character count, availability of multimedia, or privacy settings—play a subtle but critical role in shaping communication style and social norms.

- **Cultural Artifacts**

  No community is complete without its culture, and virtual communities express this through a rich tapestry of shared symbols, language, and humor. Memes, jargon, emotes, and inside jokes accumulate as cultural artifacts that foster belonging and continuity. For example, a gaming guild might use specific emotes to signal camaraderie or a coding forum might have well-known acronyms and phrases understood only by insiders.

  These artifacts are more than decoration; they function as social glue and markers of identity. Their evolution can trace a community's history and collective values. Newcomers often learn these cultural markers as a rite of passage, while long-term members may guard or adapt them to navigate changes. Importantly, these cultural products often spill beyond the community, influencing broader digital culture or inspiring creative practices.

- **Persistence and Memory**

The digital nature of virtual communities affords a remarkable capacity for persistence and memory. Discussions, files, and multimedia are archived indefinitely, searchable and retrievable long after their initial creation. This permanence creates a collective memory that shapes ongoing dialogue, references past decisions, and preserves legacy content.

Archives become repositories of community lore and knowledge, supporting newcomers and guiding future actions. However, persistence also brings challenges: old conflicts can resurface, outdated norms may clash with evolving values, and questions arise about privacy and data ownership. Managing this collective memory thoughtfully is a defining challenge as virtual communities navigate their growth and transformation over time.

21

Characteristic	Gaming Communities	Fan Forums	Professional Networks	Open Source Projects
Identity & Representation	Player tags, customizable avatars	Usernames, fan art avatars	Real names, professional photos	Handles, contribution stats
Norms & Rules	Code of conduct, fair play	Content sharing policies, spoiler warnings	Professional etiquette	Contribution guidelines, licensing terms
Member Roles	Players, guild leaders, moderators	Fans, thread starters, moderators	Members, recruiters, admins	Contributors, maintainers, moderators
Governance Structures	Clan hierarchies, developer oversight	Community-elected moderators	Corporate policies, board oversight	Meritocracy, consensus-driven
Communication Modalities	Voice chat, in-game chat, forums	Discussion boards, live chats	Emails, webinars, LinkedIn groups	Mailing lists, issue trackers, chats
Technological Infrastructure	Game servers, anti-cheat tools	Forum software, content management	Enterprise platforms, CRM	Version control, continuous integration tools
Cultural Artifacts	Game memes, emotes	Fan fiction, jargon	Industry buzzwords, certifications	Coding memes, project logos
Persistence & Memory	Match histories, replays	Thread archives, fan histories	Document repositories, archives	Code repositories, changelogs

Table 1.1: Characteristics of Various Types of Virtual Communities

1.5 How Virtual Communities Differ from Traditional Ones

Understanding the distinct qualities that separate virtual communities from their traditional, face-to-face counterparts is crucial for grasping how social bonds, interaction patterns, and collective identities evolve in the digital age. While both forms aim to foster connection and shared purpose, the environments in which they operate—one grounded in physical presence, the other dispersed across cyberspace—endow them with very different characteristics. Exploring these differences along key dimensions such as space, time, identity, and governance reveals not only how community life has adapted to technological shifts but also how these changes influence member experience and social dynamics.

Physical proximity traditionally anchors community life in localized, face-to-face settings. Neighborhoods, clubs, workplaces, and family gatherings depend on physical nearness to facilitate spontaneous encounters, shared activities, and sensory engagement. These communities manifest the tangible presence of bodies in a space, reinforcing social bonds through gestures, expressions, and direct conversation. In contrast, virtual communities transcend geography entirely. Participants connect from diverse locations, nation-states, and time zones, brought together by shared interests or goals rather than shared streets or buildings. This global reach turns locality into a flexible concept; a discussion forum for hobbyists, for instance, might include members from Tokyo, Nairobi, and São Paulo simultaneously. The absence of physical boundaries expands access and diversity, yet also reshapes the texture of social interaction from embodied presence to mediated text, audio, or video.

Alongside spatial differences, temporal rhythms divide these two forms of association. Traditional groups often coordinate around scheduled meetups—weekly book clubs, Sunday church services, or monthly neighborhood councils—that structure interactions in

23

sync with participants' daily routines. These events impose temporal constraints: attendance requires aligning calendars, and conversations flow in real time. Virtual communities, however, harness the asynchronous nature of digital platforms, allowing members to contribute, respond, and revisit discussions on their own time. A Reddit thread or a Discord channel remains active 24/7, accommodating the erratic and varied schedules of global participants. This fluid temporality increases inclusiveness, enabling engagement across different lifestyles, but can also fragment conversations, weakening the immediacy and shared experience that defines synchronous encounters.

Membership in traditional communities tends to be stable and place-based. People grow up in neighborhoods, follow long-term affiliations with workplaces or religious congregations, and often find it difficult to detach abruptly because physical ties and social expectations are intertwined. Joining or leaving a group typically involves rituals of inclusion or farewell, conferring a sense of permanence and responsibility. In contrast, virtual communities offer remarkable fluidity. Joining a forum is often a matter of creating an account; leaving can be as simple as logging off or unsubscribing, without physical obligation or social inconvenience. This ease fosters "roaming" behaviors, where individuals participate in multiple online spaces simultaneously, shifting their attention according to interest or mood. While this flexibility encourages diverse engagements, it also challenges the depth of commitment and continuity that traditional communities often rely upon.

Identity presentation reveals one of the most intriguing contrasts. In many face-to-face groups, real-name conventions and visible social cues form the bedrock of trust and accountability. Knowing someone's name, appearance, and social background anchors interactions in an established social reality. Virtual communities, meanwhile, often feature a spectrum of anonymity and pseudonymity. Users may appear under chosen handles, avatars, or profiles that obscure age, gender, or ethnicity. This can empower self-expression and protect privacy but can also introduce ambiguity and risk—both in terms of deception and in the difficulty of gauging sincerity. The flexibility of online identity challenges traditional notions of authenticity and complicates the formation of social capital, as trust must be negotiated without the usual markers of face-to-face acquaintance.

The scalability and speed at which virtual communities can grow dwarf those of traditional communities. While a neighborhood group might gradually recruit new members over months or years, an online forum can attract thousands within days, fueled by viral sharing, search engine visibility, or platform algorithms. This rapid expansion benefits niche interests or emergent causes, enabling large-scale gathering around shared passions without geographical constraints. Yet scaling up also strains social cohesion; the intimacy and familiarity of small groups can give way to dispersed networks, necessitating new forms of moderation and coordination to maintain focus and civility in sprawling communities.

The nature of resource sharing highlights another dimension of contrast. Traditional communities often exchange physical goods, services, or spaces—sharing tools, hosting meetings in living rooms, or pooling labor for communal benefit. These tangible exchanges depend on proximity and material availability. Virtual communities, lacking physical co-location, revolve around digital assets: information, multimedia content, software, and data. Sharing takes the form of posting guides, collaborative editing, or exchanging ideas instantaneously across continents. This lowers barriers to contribution and democratizes participation but also shifts the locus of value from owned objects to shared knowledge and networked interaction.

Governance structures in traditional communities typically emerge organically, grounded in local customs, face-to-face negotiations, and informal consensus. Leadership may rotate or be recognized by social standing, with norms enforced through direct social pressure and visibility. Virtual communities, by contrast, often require codified rules documented in platform policies and enforced by moderators or automated systems. This form of governance tends to be more explicit and formalized to manage larger, more anonymous membership bases, preventing spam, harassment, or off-topic behavior. While this structure provides clarity and scale, it may also feel impersonal or rigid compared to the flexible, negotiated norms of traditional groups.

Synthesizing these contrasts reveals how physicality, temporality, identity, scale, resources, and control mechanisms shape very different community experiences. Traditional communities offer embodied, time-bound interactions that cultivate enduring bonds through shared context and mutual accountability. Virtual communities provide expansive, asynchronous, and fluid environments that prioritize inclusivity, diversity, and rapid growth, but often contend with challenges of trust, identity ambiguity, and fragmented attention. Each form cultivates distinct modes of social life; understanding their differences helps us appreciate the evolving landscape of communal existence.

These distinctions carry profound implications for how

members develop trust, maintain cohesion, and foster growth. Physical proximity and real-name conventions can nurture strong interpersonal trust, while virtual anonymity requires new mechanisms such as reputation systems or platform endorsements. Temporal flexibility in virtual spaces allows communities to welcome wider participation but demands intentional efforts— like scheduled events or dedicated moderators—to weave disparate activities into coherent social fabric. The scalability of online communities enables rapid mobilization and innovation but also calls for robust governance to manage complexity. In essence, the interplay of these factors reshapes what it means to belong, collaborate, and co-create in the contemporary world, signaling ongoing transformations in human sociality as we navigate the borderlands of physical and virtual life.

1.6 Community Membership and Belonging

Becoming a member of a virtual community is much more than clicking "join" or subscribing to a forum. Membership entails an evolving relationship marked by interaction, recognition, and a shared sense of purpose. At the heart of this transformation lies a set of criteria and thresholds that distinguish casual visitors from active participants. Membership in online communities often hinges on both explicit rules—such as user registration or agreeing to community guidelines— and implicit ones, such as contribution frequency or meaningful engagement in discussions. For example, a member might be considered "active" only after posting a minimum number of comments, sharing original content, or consistently participating over time.

These thresholds serve as landmarks signaling deeper involvement, shaping both individual identity and the collective character of the group.

Understanding why people join virtual communities reveals much about how these digital spaces function. Motivations can be as varied as the communities themselves, but common drivers include information seeking, social support, and identity affirmation. Some users come in search of expertise or answers—think of a hobbyist turning to a forum for technical advice or a patient navigating a health-support group. Others seek emotional connection, camaraderie, or a safe space to share personal experiences. Finally, many join to affirm or explore aspects of their identity, finding resonance in communities centered on culture, politics, or niche interests. These motivations often overlap and evolve, reflecting individuals' changing needs and the dynamic nature of community life.

Social identity theory offers a powerful lens for understanding how a virtual community becomes "us" rather than simply "them." This theory posits that individuals categorize themselves and others into groups, which in turn shapes their self-concept and behavior. Within online communities, members experience an in-group, the collective to which they belong, and simultaneously identify others as out-group members. This distinction fosters belonging but can also generate boundaries and tensions. For instance, newcomers may initially feel like outsiders until they are assimilated into shared language, values, or rituals. Meanwhile, the in-group status can imbue members with pride and motivation to uphold community norms, reinforcing cohesion and collective identity.

Membership in virtual communities often unfolds in stages, mirroring socialization in real-world groups.

Newcomers typically start as lurkers—observing, learning the tone and culture without immediate participation. Encouraged by a welcoming environment, they might contribute sporadically, gradually becoming regular members as they engage more confidently and frequently. If sustained, this involvement can lead to veteran status, with members deeply embedded in the community's fabric. Veterans tend to possess institutional memory, exert informal leadership, and help maintain social order. This trajectory reveals the developmental nature of belonging: it is earned and cultivated through interaction rather than assumed instantly.

Effective onboarding processes are crucial for guiding newcomers into the fold. Virtual communities employ diverse rituals and mechanisms to ease this transition, such as automated welcome messages, orientation threads, or mentor pairings. These practices help demystify community norms, encourage initial participation, and convey that newcomers matter. For example, subreddit communities often have pinned posts explaining etiquette and invite new users to introduce themselves. Similarly, some platforms use customized badges or starter kits to reward first contributions, reinforcing positive engagement early on. These seemingly small acts of hospitality build rapport and lay foundations for longer-term belonging.

Longtime members play pivotal roles beyond participation, assuming responsibilities as mentors, leaders, and knowledge stewards. Veteran members often serve as guides, answering questions, clarifying norms, and modeling accepted behavior. Their presence stabilizes community dynamics, moderates conflicts, and nurtures incoming members. In some platforms, veterans formally moderate forums, curate content,

29

or organize events. More subtly, they personify the community's values and history, anchoring collective memory. This stewardship is essential, as it balances openness with continuity, helping the community maintain identity amid growth and change.

To encourage sustained engagement, online communities have devised creative mechanisms such as badges, reputation systems, and gamification. Badges may recognize milestones—completing profiles, making a certain number of posts, or receiving peer endorsements—providing visible tokens of achievement. Reputation points can incentivize quality contributions and signal trustworthiness to others. Gamification transforms participation into an enjoyable, goal-oriented experience, motivating users through challenges, leaderboards, and rewards. These tools do more than reward activity; they cultivate a sense of progress and pride, reinforcing members' emotional investment and integrating identity with participation.

The sense of belonging that arises within virtual communities is a distinctive blend of emotional attachment and group cohesion. Though mediated by screens and text, these connections can feel remarkably real and meaningful. Members often describe experiencing comfort, shared purpose, and mutual support akin to offline social bonds. This communal feeling emerges through repeated interactions, ritualized exchanges, and recognition of individuality within the collective. A key ingredient is validation—knowing that one's contributions matter and that one is accepted. Belonging thus becomes both an internal conviction and a social reality, fostering loyalty and resilience in the face of challenges.

Yet, barriers to belonging persist, complicating the ideal of inclusive communities. Exclusionary norms, whether explicit or subtle, can alienate newcomers or minority members. Language obstacles pose additional hurdles; communities dominated by a single language may unintentionally marginalize those less fluent. Cultural gaps—differences in values, humor, or communication styles—can also impede integration. Moreover, the anonymity and disinhibition online sometimes exacerbate social rifts or harassment, undermining trust and safety. Recognizing these barriers is essential, as they shape who feels welcome and who is left on the fringes.

Successful communities adopt deliberate strategies to foster belonging and nurture sustained engagement. Best practices include cultivating inclusive norms that celebrate diversity and discourage exclusion, explicitly recognizing and rewarding contributions of all members, and providing accessible onboarding that lowers entry barriers. Creating spaces for informal social interaction alongside task-focused discussions helps build rapport. Encouraging veteran members to mentor newcomers blends continuity with openness. Transparency in moderation and conflict resolution reinforces fairness and trust. Through such methods, communities transform from anonymous aggregations into genuine social ecosystems where individuals thrive together.

Community membership and belonging in virtual spaces thus embody a complex, evolving interplay of identity, motivation, social interaction, and cultural norms. Far from mere digital gatherings, these communities offer profound experiences of connection, responsibility, and shared meaning. Navigating the thresholds and pathways of membership reveals not only how individuals become part of a group, but also how groups sustain themselves and adapt through

31

continual human engagement.

Chapter 2

A Brief History of Virtual Communities

This chapter traces the evolution of online social spaces from pre–web experiments through today's global platforms. We begin with the birth of networked communication in ARPANET and early forums, then follow the rise of social networking sites, immersive gaming worlds, and mobile messaging apps. Next, we examine how communities transcended borders to become truly global, and conclude with in-depth case studies of landmark virtual communities that shaped online culture and governance.

2.1 The Early Internet and Online Forums

Long before the dazzling multimedia experiences associated with today's internet, the seeds of virtual community life were sown in a far humbler digital garden. This garden began cultivating connections in an era dominated by text, slow connections, and modest hardware but with an extraordinary spirit of collaboration and curiosity. To understand the origins of virtual communities, we must look back to the pioneering infrastructures and social experiments that preceded the World Wide Web: ARPANET, email lists, Usenet newsgroups, and Bulletin Board Systems (BBSes). Each played a crucial role in shaping the interactive spaces where people first gathered to share knowledge, debate ideas, and simply chat.

ARPANET's development in the late 1960s laid the technological and cultural groundwork. Originally funded by the U.S. Department of Defense, ARPANET was designed to connect research institutions and enable resource sharing. This network, often called the internet's great-grandfather, was revolutionary not only for linking computers but for allowing users to communicate directly. One of the earliest and most transformative applications on ARPANET was email. By the early 1970s, email had become the "killer app" of the network, facilitating instant, asynchronous communication among researchers dispersed across the country. In addition to email, ARPANET allowed file transfers, enhancing collaboration on projects by letting users share data without physical media. These advances planted the idea that networked computers could function as social tools, rather than mere computational devices.

Building upon ARPANET's email functionality, mailing lists emerged as one of the first forms of group discussion online. The introduction of LISTSERV in 1986 automated the process of managing email discussion groups, allowing users to subscribe and receive messages in a shared conversation thread. Topic-based mailing lists flourished, enabling enthusiasts from astronomy to farming to engage in extended dialogues. Unlike the more open forums of later internet days, mailing lists often had an exclusive, invitation-based feel, which fostered tightly knit communities united around shared interests. LISTSERV and its contemporaries were crucial because they provided a simple, decentralized infrastructure for community interaction, long before web browsers could render forums visually.

Around the same time, another ground-breaking platform was taking shape: Usenet. Conceived in 1979 by university students Tom Truscott and Jim Ellis, Usenet was a distributed discussion system that resembled a giant digital bulletin board. It operated on a hierarchy of newsgroups—organized by subject areas such as `comp.*`, `sci.*`, and `rec.*`—where users could post messages readable by anyone subscribed to those groups. Unlike email lists, Usenet's design promoted wide public access, allowing anyone with a connection to read and contribute. This openness gave rise to a sprawling, decentralized community where hobbies, politics, technical support, and culture collided. Usenet's threaded conversations and the sheer volume of participants generated a wild, emergent social environment, which would echo throughout later internet spaces.

While ARPANET and Usenet were primarily academic and institutional, Bulletin Board Systems (BBSes) brought early virtual communities directly into homes and local neighborhoods through dial-up modems. Flourishing in the 1980s and early 1990s, BBSes were privately run computers that users could call using a telephone line to exchange messages, download files, or play games. Each BBS had a "sysop" (system operator) who managed the site and moderated interactions, often building close relationships with regular users. BBSes introduced many enduring features of online community software: threaded messaging boards for discussions, mechanisms for file-sharing such as text files, software, and images, and "door games," interactive multiplayer games running in the background. The local and personal flavor of many BBSes cultivated intimate cultures and identities, where usernames became avatars and sites developed reputations.

Informal moderation was a key social mechanism in both BBSes and Usenet. Without sophisticated automated filters or corporate oversight, sysops and volunteer caretakers bore the responsibility for maintaining a civil and welcoming space. Their methods varied—from gentle reminders and warnings to banning disruptive users—but their authority was usually enforced by the trust and respect of the community rather than rigid rules. This grassroots approach to moderation set a precedent for later internet governance debates, highlighting early tensions between freedom of expression and community standards.

The arrival of the web around the mid-1990s marked a turning point, triggering a gradual migration from text-based protocols to browser-friendly forum platforms. Web forum software like phpBB, launched in 2000, introduced a more accessible and visually organized format for online discussions. Unlike text-based mailing lists or newsgroups, web forums allowed users to navigate easily between sections, track individual threads, and incorporate multimedia elements. This shift democratized participation further by lowering the technical barriers to entry and inviting a broader, more diverse audience to join virtual communities. The web also simplified moderation tools and user management, ushering in a new phase of scalability and complexity for online social spaces.

Technical limitations profoundly shaped early online community design. Hardware constraints meant that servers were often modest in capacity, and dial-up connections were slow and costly. Bandwidth restrictions necessitated text-heavy content and discouraged large file sharing or multimedia—most conversations relied heavily on succinct messages and ASCII art for expression. Network protocols like UUCP (Unix-to-Unix Copy Program) for Usenet or SMTP for email mailing lists were robust yet limited, emphasizing reliability over speed or graphical richness. These constraints fostered a culture of patience and considered communication, contrasting with the fast-paced immediacy of today's internet.

The social dynamics within early forums reflected the novelty and experimental nature of networked interaction. Status hierarchies emerged organically, often linked to technical prowess or longevity rather than real-world credentials. Users earned respect by helping newcomers, posting insightful content, or creating popular resources. Etiquette was communicated through community norms—questions about "netiquette" appeared early, guiding newcomers on appropriate language, formatting, and posting frequency. Avatars and pseudonyms allowed for identity play, providing a safe space for self-expression and sometimes reinvention. The relative anonymity combined with communal accountability created rich, complex interpersonal relationships.

First-generation users of these early digital communities tended to be academics, hobbyists, and technophiles—people motivated by curiosity, necessity, or the desire to connect beyond their immediate environment. They often exhibited high tolerance for technical challenges and a patient approach to communication. Demographically, these users skewed toward a younger, predominantly male population with access to universities or workplaces equipped with computing resources. Their pioneering behaviors, like chronicling digital culture or establishing moderation norms, paved the way for the explosion of online communication that followed.

Platform	Launch Year	Key Features
ARPANET	1969	Packet-switched network, early email and file transfer
LISTSERV	1986	Automated email list management, topic-based mailing lists
Usenet	1979	Distributed newsgroups, public threaded discussions
BBSes	Early 1980s	Dial-up access, sysop moderation, file sharing, door games
phpBB (Web Forums)	2000	Browser-based, multimedia support, scalable moderation

Table 2.1: Key Early Online Community Platforms and Their Features

By tracing the lineage from ARPANET through mailing lists, Usenet, BBSes, to web forums, we uncover the architectural and social scaffolding upon which today's vast virtual communities are built. These early forums combined limitations and inventiveness to cultivate spaces of shared exploration and discourse, setting enduring patterns of interaction that continue to influence how we come together online.

2.2 The Rise of Social Networks

Social network sites emerged as digital spaces where individuals could create profiles, establish connections, and share content through dynamic feeds. At their core, these platforms provided a framework to represent identity and social ties online, transforming isolated web pages into living, interactive communities. Profiles acted as personal canvases—displaying interests, photos, and status updates—while connections mapped out one's social circle, making relationships visible and navigable. Feeds aggregated friends' activities in real time, inviting continual engagement and fostering a sense of belonging. This trifecta—profiles, connections, and feeds—became the defining architecture of social networking platforms, setting the stage for their explosive growth.

The first significant attempt to realize these ideas on a large scale was *SixDegrees*, launched in 1997. It introduced users to the notion of a personal profile page complemented by a friend list, embodying the theory popularly known as *six degrees of separation*. SixDegrees allowed users to list friends and view friends-of-friends, turning the abstract concept of networks into a tangible, browsable experience. Though rudimentary by today's standards, it pioneered the essential mechanics of friend lists and profile customization. However, limited internet penetration and nascent social media culture meant SixDegrees struggled to gain lasting traction, eventually folding in 2000. Yet, it planted the critical seed: online social graphs, where relationships define navigation and interaction.

Building on these foundations, *Friendster* arrived in 2002 with vivid ambitions to become the "next big thing" in online socializing. It rapidly attracted millions, fueled by what would become a textbook example of viral growth. Early adopters enthusiastically invited their friends, who in turn invited their friends, creating a positive feedback loop that propelled Friendster's user base into the tens of millions within a year. This viral expansion revealed the sheer power of social connections as a growth engine. However, the platform soon buckled under its own success. Scalability issues plagued the infrastructure; pages grew sluggish, notifications delayed, and frustration mounted. Friendster's early story illustrates both the promise and peril of social networks—growth is necessary for relevance, yet rapid expansion demands robust backend resilience. The site's struggles underscored that user experience could not be sacrificed on the altar of ambition.

While Friendster wrestled with scale, *MySpace* emerged in 2003 and captured the zeitgeist of youth culture with striking success. Unlike its predecessors, MySpace empowered users with unprecedented profile customization—backgrounds, music playlists, embedded videos—turning pages into personal expressions and artistic showcases. This surface-level creativity dovetailed with a deep integration of music culture: unsigned artists found an audience, and fans discovered new tunes, establishing MySpace as a cultural hub. Its open architecture invited experimentation and social play, inviting users to curate their personalities while connecting with peers. The vibrant, chaotic spirit of MySpace embodied how social networks could be playgrounds for identity as much as communication tools. However, this freedom sometimes came at the cost of usability and security, foreshadowing challenges ahead.

Running parallel to these consumer-focused platforms was *LinkedIn*, established in 2003 with a distinctly pro-fessional focus. It reframed social networking through the lens of career advancement, offering tools like group discussions, job listings, and endorsements. LinkedIn's profiles emphasized professional achievements and skills, and its recommendation system added social proof to expertise. Rather than casual socializing, LinkedIn cultivated a space for strategic networking, knowledge sharing, and reputational management. It demonstrated that the model of profiles and connections could be adapted beyond personal and entertainment contexts to serve practical, career-oriented goals. This specialization helped LinkedIn carve out a durable niche among a growing ecosystem of social platforms.

The emergence of *Facebook* in 2004 marked a transformative moment that reshaped social networking into a global phenomenon. Initially restricted to Harvard students, Facebook exploited the allure of exclusivity and campus ties, creating interconnected "networks" that mirrored real-world social structures. Its clean interface and focus on real-world identity set it apart, fostering trust and authenticity. Facebook gradually expanded to other universities before opening to the public in 2006, by which time network effects were in full throttle. Each new user increased the platform's value not only for themselves but for others, accelerating adoption exponentially. Features like the News Feed, introduced in 2006, aggregated friends' activities into a continuously updated stream, encouraging frequent visits and real-time interaction. Facebook's ability to balance simplicity with innovation, while carefully refining its core features, propelled it to dominate the social networking landscape.

Central to the rapid ascent of these platforms is the concept of *network effects*—a phenomenon where the value of a service grows as more people use it. The more friends who joined a network, the more attractive it became for others, creating self-reinforcing loops of adoption and engagement. This positive feedback fueled viral growth: as users invited their contacts, connections multiplied exponentially, and the platform's social graph expanded in richness and complexity. Engagement became habitual as users monitored updates, posted content, and maintained relationships. Features such as tagging, commenting, and sharing further embedded users into dynamic social ecosystems. The network effect not only accelerated user acquisition but also entrenched platforms as essential social infrastructure, making it increasingly difficult for new entrants to compete.

However, as social networks scaled, concerns around *privacy* and data control surfaced prominently. Platforms collected vast troves of personal information—friends lists, preferences, location data—raising questions about who could access and monetize this data. Early controversies highlighted tensions between inviting sharing and protecting user agency. For example, Facebook's evolving privacy settings were often criticized for complexity and ambiguity, sometimes resulting in inadvertent exposure of personal details. Data breaches, unauthorized third-party access, and targeted advertising practices intensified scrutiny. These debates revealed the challenge of balancing personalized social experiences with safeguarding individual rights, an issue that continues to shape platform policies and user expectations.

Monetization models evolved alongside these privacy dynamics. Advertising became the dominant revenue source, with platforms leveraging detailed user data to deliver highly targeted ads. Sponsored content, promoted posts, and native advertising blurred the lines between user-generated and commercial material, raising further questions about authenticity and influence. Some platforms experimented with premium subscriptions offering enhanced features—LinkedIn's paid tiers, for instance, provided recruiters and professionals with more tools. Yet, data-driven advertising remained the primary engine, as platforms capitalized on their unique position at the intersection of personal networks and consumer markets. This economic dynamic underscored social networks not merely as communication tools but as powerful intermediaries in digital commerce.

Reflecting on the trajectory from SixDegrees to Facebook reveals enduring design patterns and cautionary tales that continue to inform social networking today. Profiles, connections, and dynamic feeds remain fundamental, while customization and platform specialization cater to diverse user needs. The imperative to build robust, scalable infrastructure became painfully clear, as did the necessity of managing network effects without compromising privacy and trust. Moreover, the delicate balance between user empowerment and commercial exploitation revealed itself as a persistent challenge. The rise of social networks is a story of rapid innovation intertwined with social complexity—demonstrating how digital platforms reshape human interaction in profound and lasting ways.

2.3 Gaming Communities and Virtual Worlds

The journey from humble text-based Multi-User Dungeons (MUDs) to sprawling graphical Massively Multiplayer Online Role-Playing Games (MMORPGs) charts a fascinating evolution of virtual sociality and immersive world-building. Originally conceived in the late 1970s and early 1980s, MUDs were the first shared digital spaces where multiple players could interact simultaneously through typed commands and descriptions. These text-only realms allowed adventurers to explore dungeons, solve puzzles, and engage with one another using nothing more than imagination and prose. The lack of graphics did not diminish their richness; instead, it amplified the players' collaborative world-building, as the scenes were painted uniquely in the mind's eye of each participant.

Social interaction in these early MUDs was fundamental to their appeal. Communication was the lifeblood, with open chat channels enabling role-play, strategic cooperation, and spontaneous storytelling. Players assumed characters with distinct personalities and histories, often governed by in-game codes of conduct or elaborate virtual governments created to manage disputes, enforce rules, and organize community life. Questing together forged bonds, while guilds and clans began to emerge as formalized collectives, laying the groundwork for structured social groupings that would define future online worlds. These communities were persistent in character, developing traditions, hierarchies, and conflict resolution strategies that mimicked real-world social governance.

As computer graphics technology advanced and internet access broadened in the 1990s, the shift from MUDs to graphical MMORPGs began in earnest. Landmark titles such as *Ultima Online* (1997) and *EverQuest* (1999) introduced visually rendered landscapes where avatars could walk, fight, trade, and socialize in real time. These games transformed the experience of virtual worlds from abstract text into immersive environments inhabited by tens of thousands of simultaneous players. The visual dimension intensified feelings of presence and identity, enabling players to express themselves not only through words but through customized appearances and in-world behaviors. The design of these spaces emphasized persistence—the game world continued to evolve and function even when individual players logged off, seeding a sense of a living, breathing community.

With the rise of graphical MMORPGs came increasingly

sophisticated social structures. Guilds and clans matured into organized institutions with formal leadership roles, membership charters, and internal rules resembling those of real organizations. Leaders coordinated raids, diplomatic relations with other groups, and resource distribution. These player-driven hierarchies supported complex social dynamics, including mentorship, conflict mediation, and political maneuvering. In many cases, leadership required not just gaming skill but social savvy and administrative talent. The formation of such bodies illustrated that virtual worlds were not just games but burgeoning societies with their own norms and governance.

Parallel to social complexity, virtual economies flourished within these persistent worlds. Game designers implemented in-game currencies, market-places, and crafting systems that mimicked economic behaviors seen offline. Players bought, sold, and bartered everything from weapons to rare artifacts, often engaging in specialized professions such as blacksmithing or alchemy. Beyond merely trading for play purposes, a fascinating phenomenon emerged: real-world money began to flow into virtual economies, with players purchasing items or accounts through third-party markets. This blurred the boundary between play and livelihood, giving rise to "gold farming" operations and debates about the value and ethics of digital goods. The rise of real-money trading highlighted the growing economic significance of virtual worlds, intersecting with broader concerns about labor, value, and regulation in digital spaces.

Communication tools likewise evolved rapidly to support these social and economic structures. Early text chat broadened into integrated voice channels, enabling instantaneous collaboration and camaraderie. As streaming platforms grew, many players began sharing their gameplay in real time with global audiences, fostering interactive communities beyond the game itself. In parallel, dedicated community hubs, forums, and content creation sites sprang up to exchange strategies, fan art, and gossip. These communication innovations transformed the solitary act of gaming into a richly networked social experience, knitting together diverse players around common interests and goals.

The core innovation sustaining these connected communities was the concept of the persistent world— a server environment that operated continuously, day and night, independent of any single player's presence. This "always-on" infrastructure meant the virtual realm existed as a stable, evolving place where players could return at any moment to find ongoing developments, player-driven events, or simply familiar faces. Persistence fostered a shared history, with evolving storylines shaped both by developers and the players themselves. It also nurtured investment in character growth and social ties, as individuals' virtual lives intertwined with real-world routines and friendships.

A vibrant feature of these persistent worlds has been the cultivation of community events. Developers and players alike organized in-game festivals, competitions, and challenges that punctuated regular gameplay with moments of collective celebration and spectacle. Player-organized gatherings, such as role-playing events or fan festivals, sometimes extended beyond the screen into real-world conventions, merging virtual and physical social spheres. These events underscored the role of games not merely as entertainment, but as cultural spaces where identity, creativity, and social bonds were expressed and ritualized.

Moreover, the culture of modding and fan-generated content extended the life and texture of MMORPGs far beyond their original design. Enthusiast communities created custom modifications, private servers, and narrative expansions, enriching the gaming experience and sometimes even influencing official game development. This participatory model showcased a profound shift toward collaborative authorship, where gamers were not just consumers but co-creators of the worlds they inhabited. Fan projects preserved and revitalized classic games, underscoring the emotional and cultural attachment players felt toward virtual worlds.

The impact of these developments has rippled well beyond the screen. Many gamers report friendships forged in virtual worlds that translate into meaningful real-life relationships. Competitive gaming communities have coalesced into professional e-sports industries, offering careers in play and spectating. The economies seeded in games have had spillover effects into technology, marketing, and digital culture. Perhaps most significantly, MMORPGs and their predecessors have demonstrated that virtual worlds are complex social ecosystems—spaces where identity, community, economy, and culture intertwine in dynamic and evolving ways.

In tracing this lineage, we see how early text-based MUDs laid the critical groundwork for understanding online interaction as a form of social experience, not just game mechanics. The transition to graphical MMORPGs layered emotive presence and intricate social systems atop this foundation, resulting in virtual worlds that are socially persistent, economically vibrant, and culturally significant. These environments continue to evolve, inviting us to reconsider the boundaries of community, economy, and identity in the digital age.

2.4 Mobile and Messaging Era

The turn of the 21st century marked a tectonic shift in how people communicate, moving from stationary web portals and traditional voice calls to an increasingly mobile, messaging-first landscape. Long before sleek apps dominated our screens, it was the humble SMS that kickstarted the networked social life of friends and families on the go. Early SMS group chats, often cobbled together by juggling contact lists and responding to threads of messages in bursts, formed informal but powerful micro-communities. These text message clusters—whether for planning weekend outings or keeping relatives connected—were the scaffolding for more sophisticated mobile social fabrics. They demonstrated the innate human desire to be "always reachable," laying the groundwork for what would soon evolve into seamless, rich-media conversations.

This transformation accelerated notably with the rise of BlackBerry Messenger (BBM) in the mid-2000s. BBM innovated beyond the basic texting experience by introducing group chat capabilities, read receipts, and delivery confirmations, features that heightened the immediacy and intimacy of conversations. Users could finally see who had viewed their messages and when, creating a new social dynamic centered around responsiveness. BBM's encryption and reliability made it a darling not just of casual users but also of professionals and enterprise environments, where secure, real-time communication was paramount. It was one of the first platforms to show that messaging was no longer a sideline to voice or email but a core channel of social and organizational life.

As smartphones matured, WhatsApp emerged as a global juggernaut, redefining messaging with ease of use and privacy at its core. Its adoption of end-to-end encryption guaranteed that conversations were secure, fostering trust among billions of users worldwide. WhatsApp's support for multimedia sharing—photos, videos, voice notes, locations—transformed chats into rich, vivid interactions. No longer confined to 160-character text bursts, users could weave complex narratives and emotions within their messages. WhatsApp's ubiquity, spanning continents and cultures, illustrates how mobile-first design combined with privacy-conscious engineering can build communities transcending language and geography, where a single group chat can coordinate family gatherings, support social movements, or run microbusinesses.

Parallel to WhatsApp's global sweep was the rise of China's WeChat, which pushed the messaging envelope far beyond conversation alone. WeChat evolved into a multifunctional platform integrating payments, mini-programs, and social feeds, effectively becoming a mobile operating system inside a single app. Users don't just chat—they shop, pay bills, book appointments, and engage with branded content all without ever leaving the app environment. This integration illustrated how messaging apps could transcend communication to anchor digital life in one seamless experience. The fusion of chat and commerce transformed communities into ecosystems where social bonds and economic transactions coexist fluidly, reshaping not only social interaction but also entire business models.

Privacy concerns and customization needs led to the emergence of Telegram, championing secret chats with self-destructing messages and resilient encryption protocols. Telegram's openness—via bots and an open API—invited developers and communities to innovate on top of its basic messaging infrastructure. This created hybrid ecosystems blending automated workflows, personalized content streams, and interactive group dynamics. Telegram's approach highlighted a new era where messaging platforms became not only social tools but programmable spaces, where communities could build tailored experiences that combined chat with information distribution, event coordination, and even activism.

A key catalyst in enriching mobile messaging has been the advent of push notifications. These real-time alerts broke the boundaries of passive communication, transforming phones into ever-pulsing hubs of attention. By delivering messages instantly, notifications created a sense of presence and urgency that encouraged faster responses and sustained engagement. They changed user behavior from occasional check-ins into continuous, lightweight interactions, fostering always-on relationships. This dynamic generated new challenges—such as notification overload—and pushed designers to balance immediacy with user control, but its impact on retention and community vibrancy has been undeniable.

Simultaneously, the workplace and hobbyist spheres found new homes in chat-centric platforms like Slack and Discord. Slack revolutionized professional collaboration by structuring communication into channels, threading conversations, and integrating with countless productivity tools. It replaced sprawling email chains with focused, searchable dialogues, accelerating teamwork and flattening organizational barriers. Discord, initially popular among gamers, grew into a versatile community hub hosting groups around diverse interests, from book clubs to coding cohorts. Its voice chat rooms, real-time moderation tools, and rich social features fostered vibrant, persistent communities that thrived on interaction flexibility. Together, these platforms illustrate how messaging has evolved into specialized ecosystems tailored for work, play, and shared passions.

Another notable innovation in the mobile messaging saga is ephemeral messaging, epitomized by Snapchat. The appeal of messages that vanish—the digital equivalent of fleeting spoken words—captured a desire for spontaneity and impermanence in social interaction. Disappearing content reduces audience pressure and permanence, encouraging authenticity and playful experimentation. This shift defied traditional notions of archiving communication, emphasizing momentary connection over digital legacy. Beyond personal chats, ephemeral messaging sparked creativity in marketing and storytelling, underlining how evolving communication norms adapt to cultural shifts and privacy expectations.

Designing for these mobile and messaging-first experiences required a fundamental rethink of user interfaces and engagement strategies. Mobile-first design principles optimize for small screens, limited attention spans, and intermittent connectivity. Simplified navigation, large touch targets, and minimalistic layouts allow users to engage effortlessly while on the move. Features like typing indicators, read receipts, and inline media enrich the conversation without overwhelming the interface. Meanwhile, latency minimization and offline message caching ensure seamless interaction regardless of network conditions. By prioritizing these elements, messaging apps create intuitive and responsive experiences that match the rhythms of modern life.

Underlying these technological and design developments is a profound shift in how people engage socially. Earlier internet forums and bulletin boards operated on an asynchronous model—users posted messages and awaited responses over minutes or hours, fostering thoughtful but slow-paced discourse. Mobile messaging, by contrast, privileges immediacy and constant connectivity, where conversations unfold dynamically, message by message, across days or even moments. This always-on interaction shapes community behavior, nurturing intimacy and integration into daily routines. At the same time, it demands new norms for presence, availability, and conversational boundaries, reflecting the evolving nature of human connection in a digitally mediated world.

Together, these threads showcase how the mobile and messaging era transformed communication from momentary texts to rich, multifunctional ecosystems. From the early days of SMS group chats to today's versatile platforms like WeChat, Slack, and Telegram, the trajectory reveals a relentless drive toward connectivity that is private, immediate, interactive, and deeply embedded in everyday life. Messaging now does more than facilitate conversation—it shapes culture, commerce, and collaboration in ways that continue to surprise and redefine what community means in a mobile world.

2.5 Globalization of Community

The digital age has ushered in a remarkable transformation: communities once bound by geography now stretch effortlessly across the globe. Virtual communities—spaces where individuals gather online around shared interests, professions, or values—have evolved from niche forums into vast, international networks. Yet this expansion introduces a complex web of linguistic, cultural, logistical, and legal challenges, reshaping how people connect and govern themselves in a borderless world.

One of the most fundamental hurdles in global community-building is *language*. Early online forums operated primarily in a few dominant tongues, but a truly global platform demands support across hundreds of languages. Modern virtual spaces employ a combination of automated translation tools and sophisticated localization workflows to bridge these gaps. Machine translation engines like Google Translate or DeepL offer near-instant conversion of content, making discussion threads and announcements accessible to diverse audiences. However, the nuances of meaning, idioms, and cultural references often require human intervention. This is where crowd-sourced efforts shine: communities enlist multilingual volunteers to refine translations, adapting tone and context for accuracy and inclusiveness. Projects such as Wikipedia exemplify this model, where contributors worldwide collaboratively ensure content is not only translated but culturally resonant. Through this synergy of technology and human insight, multilingual platforms enable participation that feels native rather than foreign.

Yet language is only the beginning. Beyond communication lies the rich terrain of *cultural exchange*. Various forums and applications have emerged explicitly to encourage intercultural dialogue, turning the internet into a vibrant marketplace of ideas, customs, and worldviews. Platforms like Couchsurfing offer virtual and physical spaces where people share travel stories, recipes, and cultural festivals, fostering mutual understanding. More focused communities—such as language exchange apps like Tandem and HelloTalk—pair users eager to learn a new language with native speakers, creating a dynamic environment for both linguistic and cultural immersion. These spaces nurture empathy and curiosity, softening the boundaries that geography once imposed and showcasing the intricacies of global human connection.

In this context, *diaspora communities* have found especially fertile ground for maintaining their identities and traditions. Migrant and expatriate groups often struggle with physical distance from their homelands, but virtual platforms help bridge that gap. Facebook groups, WhatsApp circles, and specialized forums become digital town squares where news from home circulates, cultural celebrations are organized, and support networks flourish. For instance, the global Indian diaspora frequently uses platforms like WhatsApp and Telegram to coordinate festivals such as Diwali, sharing recipes, prayers, and greetings. Similarly, Syrian expatriates use online channels to stay politically engaged, exchange resources, and preserve their cultural heritage amid displacement. The internet thus transforms into a lifeline for cultural continuity, intersecting personal identity with global connectivity.

However, no global community can ignore the practical challenge of *time zones*. When members are scattered from San Francisco to Singapore, synchronous interaction—video calls, live discussions, collaborative coding sprints—requires thoughtful coordination. Communities employ a range of strategies to accommodate diverse schedules:

- Rotating meeting times to distribute inconvenience fairly;

- Asynchronous communication channels such as forums and messaging boards that allow participants to contribute at their own pace;

- Automated tools that display event times adjusted to each user's local time.

Platforms like Slack and Discord integrate "time zone bots" that help schedule meetings without confusion. While these strategies do not erase the friction of distance, they reduce barriers and respect participants' temporal realities, fostering participation without burnout.

The diversity of cultures and legal environments also demands *localized moderation* approaches. What one culture views as acceptable discourse may be taboo or offensive in another. Community guidelines, therefore, cannot be a one-size-fits-all model; they must be sensitive to varied norms while upholding core principles such as respect and safety. Moderation teams often comprise volunteers from different regions who understand the specific cultural context and can mediate conflicts thoughtfully. Larger platforms integrate localized content policies that adapt to regional sensibilities without compromising universal standards. This balancing act is delicate: too rigid an enforcement risks alienation, while too lenient an approach can breed harmful behavior. Success comes from combining automated filters, human judgment, and transparent governance to create spaces where all feel welcome.

Overlaying these cultural and operational challenges is the complex maze of *regulatory diversity*. Internet communities operate across borders, yet national laws vary dramatically on privacy, speech, and data governance. The European Union's General Data Protection Regulation (GDPR) exemplifies a sweeping framework compelling platforms to safeguard personal data and provide user control, influencing global best practices. Meanwhile, autocratic regimes impose censorship regimes requiring platforms to filter or block content deemed politically sensitive. Navigating such divergent frameworks compels platform operators to implement region-specific controls—sometimes fragmenting the user experience—while striving to maintain a cohesive global community. The tension between openness and compliance shapes which voices flourish or falter in the digital public square.

Beyond social networks, the globalization of community manifests powerfully in *open-source collaboration*. Developer communities working on projects like Linux, Python, or Mozilla Firefox epitomize large-scale, cross-border cooperation driven by shared goals rather than geography. Contributions pour in from programmers in every time zone, with governance structures that balance meritocracy and inclusivity. Distributed version control systems and asynchronous communication platforms allow teams to code, review, and iterate continuously, despite vast distances. This model has seeded innovation not only in software but also in community governance, demonstrating how global coordination can thrive with adaptable processes and clear collective purpose.

Central to these technological and social adaptations is the imperative of *inclusive design practices*. Accessibility cannot be an afterthought if communities aim for true global reach. Platforms incorporate standards that address diverse abilities—such as screen reader compatibility, adjustable fonts, and colorblind-friendly palettes—

and ensure UI/UX choices reflect cultural sensitivities, including date formats, color symbolism, and navigation metaphors. For example, a red color may signify celebration in one culture but warning in another. Thoughtful design anticipates user diversity from the outset, reducing friction and enabling a broader range of participants to contribute meaningfully.

This spirit of inclusivity feeds further into *cross-border collaboration* beyond socializing and coding, extending to academic, volunteer, and humanitarian networks. International research consortia leverage digital platforms to share data and debate theories, unbounded by physical constraints. Volunteer portals connect skilled individuals with causes worldwide—from disaster relief coordination to educational outreach—creating a tapestry of collaborative goodwill. For instance, Ushahidi, a crowdsourcing platform born in Kenya, harnesses community input from around the world to map crises and deliver aid effectively. These networks illustrate how the global community paradigm can mobilize collective intelligence and altruism at an unprecedented scale.

As virtual communities expand into global phenomena, *patterns of scale, governance, and cohesion* begin to emerge. Managing millions of users demands layered leadership, delegation, and algorithmic support to maintain order and engagement. Communities often grow federated, with localized groups linked through overarching principles and shared infrastructures. This modular architecture balances autonomy and coordination, allowing diverse cultural expressions while preserving a cohesive identity. Governance evolves from rigid top-down control toward more participatory, transparent models that reflect the pluralistic makeup of users. The challenge is continuous: scaling community spirit without diluting it, ensuring trust and inclusivity amid global diversity.

In sum, the globalization of community is a dynamic, multi-faceted process that transcends language barriers, cultural boundaries, temporal divides, and regulatory complexities. It demands innovative technological supports, flexible social norms, and conscientious governance. When navigated thoughtfully, this global tapestry enriches individual experience and collective intelligence alike—heralding a future where community is truly worldwide, yet deeply human at its core.

2.6 Examples of Influential Online Communities

Selecting exemplary online communities to study is both an art and a science. The ones discussed here—Reddit, Wikipedia, GitHub, Stack Overflow, and Ravelry—were chosen because each embodies distinctive governance structures, cultural norms, and social impacts that illuminate how virtual spaces evolve, sustain themselves, and influence the wider world. Together, they offer a rich spectrum: from sprawling, loosely controlled forums to tightly curated knowledge repositories and specialized niche networks. Their stories reveal the delicate balance between user autonomy and centralized oversight, the dynamics of collective knowledge creation, and the economic underpinnings that support virtual social ecosystems.

Reddit: A Digital Town Square Built on Subreddit Autonomy

Reddit sprang to life in 2005 as a general-purpose aggregator, a place where users could share links and discuss virtually any topic. Its core innovation was the introduction of *subreddits*: user-created, theme-specific communities nested within the larger platform. These subreddits range from the wildly popular (r/technology, r/funny) to the hyper-niche (r/leftsharks, a subreddit devoted to a band's mascot). This modular structure fosters diversity while maintaining coherence under the Reddit umbrella.

Central to Reddit's experience is the voting mechanism—upvotes and downvotes—which collectively determine the prominence of posts and comments. This democratic element incentivizes quality and relevance, though it is not without flaws. Popular opinions often bubble to the surface, while minority voices may struggle for visibility, raising questions about the platform's representativeness and echo chambers.

Governance on Reddit: Moderators, Rules, and the Invisible Hand

The governance of Reddit rests on a layered system. Subreddit moderators are volunteers tasked with enforcing community-specific rules and mediating disputes. Given the sheer volume of activity, these moderators wield significant influence but operate without official employment or monetary rewards. Their stewardship shapes whether a subreddit remains welcoming or descends into chaos.

Above these moderators stand Reddit's administrators—the paid staff who set platform-wide policies and intervene in extreme situations such as coordinated harassment or illegal content. This duality creates a hybrid model: decentralized autonomy within subreddits combined with centralized authority at the platform level. The success of this model depends heavily on trust between users, moderators, and the platform, as well as evolving guidelines responsive to shifting social norms.

Wikipedia: The Encyclopedia Anyone Can Edit

Wikipedia embodies the wiki principle—an open collaboration model where anyone with internet access can create or edit content. This radical transparency and inclusivity have turned it into one of the most comprehensive knowledge bases in human history. Central to Wikipedia's editorial philosophy is the *neutral-point-of-view* (NPOV) policy, mandating that articles present information fairly, without bias or editorializing.

The wiki model transforms the act of knowledge creation into a social process, negotiating facts across diverse contributors. This democratization challenges traditional authority, emphasizing process over pedigree, yet it requires constant vigilance to avoid misinformation, vandalism, and bias creep.

Wikipedia's Evolving Governance: Admins, Policies, and Consensus

To manage these complexities, Wikipedia employs a structured governance framework. Volunteer administrators possess special technical privileges to protect pages and block disruptive users. Disputes often escalate to community discussions, where consensus, not majority rule, guides decisions. Policies and guidelines themselves are living documents, shaped through debate and revision.

This participatory governance fosters a culture of accountability but also exposes tensions—between openness and control, speed and accuracy, inclusivity and expertise. Wikipedia's experience demonstrates that sustaining a credible, large-scale collaborative project demands not just code but continuous social negotiation.

GitHub: The Social Fabric of Open Source Software

GitHub redefined software development by integrating *version control*—systems that track changes in code—with social networking features. Central to its model are *pull requests*, where contributors propose code changes that repository maintainers review and merge if acceptable. This mechanism enables distributed collaboration, turning software development into a public, transparent dialogue.

Forking projects to create derivative versions encourages experimentation and innovation but also raises questions about maintaining coherence and managing competing versions. Issue tracking and continuous integration (CI) services embedded within GitHub streamline not only coding but testing and deployment, reinforcing its role as a comprehensive development platform.

GitHub and the Economics of Open Source Communities

Beyond technical tools, GitHub has cultivated an ecosystem where social capital translates into tangible support. Features like sponsorship programs and marketplace integrations allow developers to monetize their work or receive funding from patrons. This soft economy underpins a vast open source infrastructure critical to the modern internet, illustrating how communal labor and market incentives coexist.

The platform's success hinges on balancing openness—forging a vibrant community of contributors—with structuring formal roles for project maintainers who steward quality and direction, a governance dance reflecting broader questions about participation and leadership in digital spaces.

Stack Overflow: Crowd-Sourced Expertise for Developers

Stack Overflow revolutionized problem-solving for programmers by creating a question-and-answer (Q&A) platform governed by reputation points and community moderation. Users gain points and privileges by providing helpful answers, encouraging quality contributions and self-regulation. Tags classify questions, enabling experts to find and answer queries in their domain.

This gamified structure converts passive knowledge consumers into active contributors, resulting in a vast, searchable trove of practical solutions. The site's architecture nurtures expertise and mentorship, democratizing access to technical help in ways traditional forums struggled to achieve.

Stack Overflow's Role in Shaping Learning and Development Workflows

The influence of Stack Overflow extends beyond answering isolated questions. It has reshaped how developers learn and work, making real-time problem-solving integral to programming. Its success also raises challenges—overly rigid norms can discourage novice participation, and reliance on crowd-sourced knowledge shifts the locus of authority from formal education to peer validation.

Nevertheless, Stack Overflow exemplifies how carefully engineered incentives and community norms convert individual contributions into communal knowledge assets, fostering an environment of continuous, distributed learning.

Ravelry: A Cozy Corner for Creative Crafting

Ravelry is a social network designed around knitters, crocheters, and fiber enthusiasts. Unlike the broad appeal of platforms like Reddit or GitHub, Ravelry thrives on its niche focus, offering rich features such as project tracking, pattern libraries, forums, and marketplace integration. Its interface encourages sharing work-in-progress photos, exchanging tips, and celebrating community milestones.

This specialized focus fosters a tight-knit culture with shared values, proving that deep engagement can flourish within bounded thematic spaces tailored to specific interests.

Ravelry's Freemium Model: Balancing Community and Commerce

While Ravelry is free to join, it incorporates a freemium model where users can purchase patterns, premium content, or merchant services. This blend of community building and commercial activity exemplifies how niche virtual spaces navigate sustainability without compromising social interactions.

Ravelry's experience highlights the potential for carefully tailored monetization strategies enabling vibrant, supportive communities that also serve practical economic functions.

Comparing Governance and Engagement Across Communities

Examining these diverse cases reveals a spectrum of governance models—from Reddit's polycentric moderator ecosystems to Wikipedia's consensus-driven policy frameworks, from GitHub's meritocratic role distinctions to Stack Overflow's gamified reputation system, and Ravelry's niche-specific, hybrid commercial-community approach. Each balances openness and control in ways shaped by its users, goals, and technological affordances.

Engagement strategies vary accordingly: collective

editing versus moderated discussion, reputation incentives versus volunteer stewardship, broad topical coverage versus focused interest groups. Sustainability depends not only on governance but on fostering social norms, shared purpose, and viable economic mechanisms.

Collectively, these communities teach that successful on-line spaces are not merely technological platforms but emergent social organisms—adaptive, negotiated, and deeply human. They remind us that virtual connections shape real-world knowledge, creativity, and culture in profound and evolving ways.

Chapter 3

How Virtual Communities Form and Grow

In this chapter, we explore the lifecycle of virtual communities from inception through maturity. We begin by examining how shared interests and identities spark new groups, then analyze the roles, rules, and governance structures that sustain them. We address strategies for recruiting and onboarding newcomers, survey the communication tools that enable interaction, illustrate how rituals and cultural practices forge cohesion, and conclude with methods for sustaining engagement and managing growth at scale.

3.1 Building a Foundation: Shared Interest and Identity

At the heart of every thriving community lies a shared focus—a domain or problem so compelling that it draws individuals together, shaping the group's raison d'être. This shared interest acts like a gravitational force, uniting people who might otherwise remain isolated in their pursuits. Whether it is amateur astronomers pooling their telescopic sightings, activists rallying around environmental protection, or enthusiasts swapping culinary secrets, the clarity of purpose provides a magnetic core. Such a unifying cause must resonate strongly enough to inspire participation and commitment, shaping the community's initial contours and fueling momentum.

This sense of unity is often articulated through carefully crafted mission statements and vision declarations. These formal expressions serve as navigational beacons that align efforts and aspirations. A mission statement succinctly captures the "what" and "why" of the community's existence, providing both motivation and a yardstick against which decisions are measured. Accompanying visions cast a horizon of possibility, imagining where collective action might lead. By externalizing purpose in this way, communities convert abstract intentions into concrete commitments, offering members a shared roadmap and a sense of direction even amid uncertainty.

Motivations to join and sustain engagement in communities are diverse but surprisingly consistent across contexts. A primary driver is the pursuit of knowledge exchange—individuals seek to learn from one another, contributing expertise and gaining insights impossible to achieve alone. Beyond practical learning, communities fulfill social and psychological needs: offering belonging, emotional support, and a venue for identity affirmation. This dimension is vital; being part of a community confirms one's values and worldview. It creates a social mirror that validates personal beliefs through collective endorsement, transforming isolated interests into lived identities.

The psychological underpinnings of community formation can be explored through *social identity theory*, which elucidates how people define themselves in relation to groups. Individuals categorize themselves

and others into "in-groups" and "out-groups," finding
self-esteem in their affiliative bonds and often marking
boundaries that differentiate insiders from outsiders.
This self-categorization process generates a shared
sense of "we"—a collective identity that evolves not
just by what members share internally but also by how
they distinguish themselves externally. Such dynamics
influence everything from group loyalty to the way
communities handle conflict and change.

Closely related to this is the concept of *affinity spaces*,
informal environments where participation is driven
by shared interests rather than formal membership
or credentials. Affinity spaces—whether a local skate
park, an online forum dedicated to vintage video
games, or a knitting circle—promote learning and
collaboration through voluntary engagement. They
emphasize accessibility and collective knowledge-
building, allowing newcomers and experts to coexist
and contribute in meaningful ways. These spaces
demonstrate that community is as much about cultural
connection and shared passion as it is about structured
organization.

Communities do not merely exist; they thrive through
continuous exchange of value. This *value exchange*
takes many forms: experts offer knowledge and
guidance, building reputations and social capital;
novices gain skills and feedback; all members receive
emotional support that sustains ongoing involvement.
Importantly, these exchanges are reciprocal. A
community survives on the mutual recognition of
benefits, which encourages cooperation and collective
responsibility. The balance of giving and receiving
reinforces trust, cultivating a fertile ground for
collaboration and innovation.

Over time, a shared language emerges as a powerful tool

for building identity and cohesion. Specialized jargon, acronyms, idiomatic expressions, and symbols become a kind of verbal architecture, enabling efficient communication and signaling membership. These linguistic markers encapsulate complex concepts and histories, creating shorthand that deepens internal bonds while delineating the community from outsiders. For example, the distinct vocabulary of open-source software developers or the unique slang within a fan fiction community both serve as badges of belonging and gateways to inclusion.

Founding narratives, or origin stories, play a pivotal role in strengthening group identity. These stories recount how the community came into being—the challenges faced, the pivotal moments, the personalities involved. Like a collective myth, the founding narrative provides a shared heritage that members can reference and celebrate. It fosters pride and continuity, giving newcomers a sense of place within a historical lineage. Whether it is the tale of a grassroots collective starting in a garage or an online gaming clan overcoming early setbacks, these stories embed values and mores crucial to the community's culture.

Communities also rely on *group boundaries* to maintain coherence and identity. These boundaries may be explicit, such as eligibility criteria and rules of membership, or implicit, shaped by norms, rituals, and shared expectations. Boundaries help guide who is included and how, providing clarity that prevents dilution of purpose while managing diversity within the group. The fluidity or rigidity of these boundaries affects the community's openness and adaptability—too strict, and the group risks insularity; too loose, and it may struggle to sustain focus and trust.

Finally, the lifecycle of community development can be understood through adapted versions of Tuckman's classic stages: *forming, storming, norming*, and *performing*. In digital settings, these stages are refracted through unique challenges and opportunities brought on by virtual interaction. Initially, members test the waters and explore common interests (forming). Disagreements and power dynamics soon surface (storming), requiring negotiation and conflict resolution. Successful communities then establish shared norms, roles, and practices (norming), fostering stability. Ultimately, the group achieves effective collaboration and goal fulfillment (performing). Recognizing these phases aids in anticipating hurdles and nurturing resilient communities.

Together, these elements—shared interest, articulated purpose, motivational dynamics, identity processes, affinity spaces, reciprocal value, common language, founding myths, boundary definitions, and developmental stages—compose the bedrock upon which communities build durable, vibrant connections. They transform individual passions into collective strength, shaping social landscapes where diverse people unite, learn, and thrive.

3.2 Roles, Rules, and Governance

Communities, whether they gather in bustling town squares or digital forums, thrive on structure. This structure depends deeply on how roles are defined, rules are established, and governance is enacted. Without these, order and fairness become elusive, and the community risks fragmentation or stagnation. Exploring these intertwined elements clarifies how communities self-organize, adapt, and endure.

At the heart of any community's organization lie roles—

69

formal and informal—that members adopt. Formal roles often emerge through explicit designation: founders who initiate the community's vision, moderators who oversee day-to-day interactions, and contributors who provide content or labor that fuels the collective effort. For instance, founders often shape a community's initial character and core principles, crafting its purpose and the boundaries within which it operates. Moderators, conversely, serve as guardians of those principles, balancing the encouragement of participation with the mitigation of disruptive behavior. Contributors form the lifeblood of engagement, sharing ideas, feedback, or creative work that sustains the community's vibrancy.

Yet roles in communities are rarely static or rigid. They exist on a spectrum, reflecting both participation and influence. Many members begin as *lurkers*, quietly observing discussions or absorbing information without active involvement. These silent participants provide an essential audience that shapes norms and expectations through their collective presence. Moving along the spectrum, active but occasional contributors engage sporadically, offering comments, questions, or occasional content. At the core lie dedicated contributors and emergent leaders—individuals whose sustained commitment and expertise gradually grant them informal authority and recognition. Emergent leaders often gain influence not by appointment but through the trust and respect they earn, subtly guiding community norms and decisions.

Central to maintaining order are the responsibilities entrusted to moderators and administrators. Their duties extend beyond simply deleting inappropriate posts or banning troublemakers. Effective moderation involves careful content curation—ensuring that discussions remain relevant, respectful, and valuable. They mediate conflicts by facilitating dialogue, tempering heated exchanges, and clarifying misunderstandings before they escalate. Moreover, moderators enforce policies, interpreting rules contextually and applying sanctions when necessary to sustain fairness and collective well-being. In many ways, they act as both referees and caretakers, balancing rule enforcement with the community's social fabric.

Rules themselves operate at multiple levels, shaping behavior through a combination of explicit and implicit guidance. Explicit, codified rules are documented and communicated clearly—such as prohibitions against harassment or spam—and set firm boundaries that all members are expected to follow. Complementing these are community norms: unwritten customs that evolve organically and govern everyday etiquette, like the tone of responses or the degree of formality in interactions. These norms often have a subtler but equally powerful influence, as members internalize expected behaviors and enforce them socially. Beyond the community's self-generated guidelines are platform policies—rules set by the larger environment hosting the community, such as terms of service or content standards imposed by social media companies or forum software providers. The interplay between these rule types creates a rich regulatory landscape balancing internal autonomy and external constraints.

Governance structures provide the frameworks through which rules are enacted and revised, and roles are coordinated. Communities experiment with various models, ranging from centralized to decentralized, or hybrid forms. Centralized governance concentrates authority in a few individuals or a formal council, streamlining decision-making and providing clear accountability. This approach often emerges in smaller

71

or newer communities needing firm direction and quick responses. On the opposite end are decentralized governance models that distribute power more evenly among members, fostering participatory decision-making and collective ownership. Such models suit communities valuing inclusivity and resilience but can face challenges in coordination and consistency. Hybrid models blend these, delegating certain authorities while preserving spaces for communal input, adapting to the community's evolving needs and scale.

How decisions are made within these governance structures varies significantly, reflecting differing priorities and cultures. Consensus-building aims for collective agreement, encouraging dialogue until most members support a proposal. While inclusive and democratic, this method can be time-consuming and may stall under contentious issues. Voting mechanisms, whether direct or representative, quantify member preferences, providing clearer outcomes but sometimes at the expense of minority voices. Top-down decisions, where leaders or administrators set policies unilaterally, enhance efficiency but risk alienating the broader membership if perceived as overbearing. Many communities blend these processes, choosing the appropriate method for each type of decision—from routine moderation policies to fundamental changes in community purpose.

Enforcement mechanisms serve as the gears turning governance into practice. Automated moderation tools—such as algorithms flagging abusive language or spam—offer scalable, consistent intervention but can lack nuance and sometimes misjudge context. Reputation systems assign scores or badges to members based on their behavior and contributions, incentivizing positive participation and signaling trustworthiness.

Manual review remains crucial in complex cases requiring human judgment, balancing fairness with enforcement. The combination of these tools enables communities to manage behavior proactively, handling routine infractions swiftly while preserving space for personalized interventions.

Conflicts are inevitable in dynamic communities, but how they are resolved reveals much about governance maturity. Mediation is commonly employed to facilitate communication between disputing parties, seeking mutual understanding and resolution without formal penalties. Arbitration introduces an impartial third party who reviews evidence and issues binding decisions, useful when mediation stalls or stakes are high. Appeals procedures provide members with recourse to challenge decisions, fostering accountability and trust in governance. These layered approaches help communities maintain social cohesion, reduce resentment, and signal commitment to fairness.

No community's rules are ever truly fixed; they evolve as circumstances change. Policy evolution is a natural response to growth, shifting member demographics, emerging technologies, or novel challenges. New rules may be introduced to address unforeseen behaviors, while outdated guidelines are revised or retired. For example, the rise of new communication modes—like live streaming or ephemeral messaging—may require reconsideration of moderation priorities and tools. Communities that remain adaptive in their governance are better equipped to balance consistency with responsiveness, preserving relevance and trust over time.

As communities grow, governance faces new scalability challenges. Small groups can rely on informal norms and interpersonal knowledge to govern effectively, but larger communities require more formalized systems to maintain order and fairness. Coordination costs increase, conflicts become more complex, and member diversity broadens, testing the inclusiveness of decision-making processes. Effective strategies include delegation of authority to subgroups, modular rule sets tailored to different areas, and leveraging technology to automate routine tasks. Successful scalability strikes a balance between preserving the community's founding spirit and introducing necessary formalities to cope with complexity.

Through the careful definition of roles, thoughtful establishment of rules, and adaptive governance practices, communities cultivate environments where individuals can coexist productively. These frameworks—dynamic and negotiated—sustain order while allowing the creativity, diversity, and engagement that make communities vibrant and enduring. The intricate dance of roles, rules, and governance thus lies at the core of collective human endeavor, shaping how we come together, communicate, and grow.

3.3 Recruiting and Welcoming New Members

The vitality of any community depends on its ability to attract new members and integrate them seamlessly into its culture. Recruiting and welcoming newcomers is not merely about adding numbers; it is about creating an inviting environment that motivates early engagement and fosters lasting connections. This process begins with understanding the diverse audiences communities hope to engage and continues through thoughtful, intentional strategies that reduce friction and spark enthusiasm.

Defining and Understanding the Audience

Successful recruitment starts with clearly defining the target segments. Communities flourish when they align their values and offerings with the interests and needs of specific groups—whether hobbyists, professionals, activists, or learners. Understanding these audiences involves more than demographics; it requires insight into their preferences, motivations, and barriers to participation. For instance, a coding forum might distinguish between novices, experienced developers, or educators, tailoring outreach and onboarding to resonate with their unique challenges and goals.

By comprehensively mapping what these potential members seek—be it social connection, knowledge exchange, or career growth—communities can craft messages and environments that speak directly to them. This alignment lays the foundation for recruitment efforts that feel personal and relevant rather than generic or scattershot.

Strategic Outreach and Recruitment Channels

With a clear audience in view, the next step leverages targeted outreach strategies to capture attention and invite participation. Social media campaigns tailored to the platforms frequented by target groups can spark organic interest. Human storytelling, showcasing authentic member experiences, often outperforms sterile advertisements in conveying community value.

Partnerships with aligned organizations or influencers can amplify reach, lending credibility and access to established networks. For example, an environmental advocacy group might collaborate with schools or eco-focused brands to tap into engaged audiences. Furthermore, enabling organic discovery through search engine optimization and content seeding ensures newcomers can find the community naturally when seeking related topics.

Each outreach channel should complement the others while respecting the cultural tone and expectations of the target group—crafting invitations that feel like genuine welcome arms rather than intrusive sales pitches.

Clear and Inviting Entry Points

Recruitment efforts culminate in well-designed entry points that convert curiosity into commitment. Landing pages, sign-up flows, and invitation mechanisms function as the community's gateway; their clarity and friendliness directly impact newcomers' decisions to join.

Optimized landing pages foreground community purpose, benefits, and social proof (like testimonials or active member counts) without overwhelming visitors with information. Minimal, jargon-free sign-up forms with visible privacy assurances lower psychological barriers.

Invitations—whether sent via email, direct message, or public call-outs—should include clear calls-to-action and simple instructions for next steps. Offering multiple entry points caters to diverse preferences: some may prefer instant sign-up from a webpage, others a thoughtful invitation embedded in content or personal connection.

Onboarding That Guides Without Overwhelming

Once inside, the onboarding experience shapes newcomers' perceptions and sets the trajectory for continued involvement. Effective onboarding balances thorough orientation with respect for individual pacing, offering just enough guidance to build confidence without stifling exploration.

Components such as concise tutorials, orientation threads, and dynamic FAQs demystify the community's norms, tools, and etiquette. Guided tours or step-by-step introductions—sometimes gamified—invite active participation and familiarize members with key features. Providing easily accessible help channels reassures newcomers that support is available whenever needed.

Notably, the tone of onboarding matters: warm, approachable language encourages newcomers, while bureaucratic or rigid instruction risks alienation.

Rituals That Make Newcomers Visible and Valued

Welcoming rituals cement newcomers' sense of belonging by making their arrival visible and celebrated. Personalized welcome messages—whether automated or human-generated—express appreciation and set a positive tone. Public introductions, such as dedicated forum threads or shout-outs, invite existing members to acknowledge and engage with newcomers.

Tokens such as newcomer badges or temporary profile tags signal inclusion while gently encouraging participation in early activities. These rituals do more than mark entrance; they weave new members into the social fabric, reducing feelings of anonymity or isolation that often lead to attrition.

Mentorship: Building Bridges Within

Mentorship and buddy systems have historic roots in guilds, fraternities, and apprenticeship models, underscoring the enduring power of one-on-one support. Assigning new members a seasoned community mentor accelerates acclimation by providing personalized answers, encouragement, and social connection.

Mentors act as cultural interpreters, offering insights on norms that are rarely codified but essential to integration. Early conversations or check-ins can address doubts before they fester into disengagement. Importantly, successful programs match mentors and mentees by interests and personalities, fostering genuine relationships rather than formal obligations.

This investment in human connection often generates strong emotional bonds, anchoring newcomers to the community's life.

Activating New Members Through Meaningful Early Actions

Research in community psychology reveals that members' early behaviors significantly predict long-term retention. Activation thresholds denote those key actions that help newcomers feel invested and competent—whether it is posting a first message, completing a profile, or responding to a poll.

Facilitating low-barrier initial contributions builds momentum. For instance, inviting new members to participate in a poll, comment on a thread, or share a brief introduction lowers the stakes of engagement and avoids intimidation. Each small success fosters confidence and demonstrates that the community values their voice.

Communities that actively encourage and recognize these early contributions not only increase participation but create a snowball effect of ongoing involvement.

Feedback Loops That Reinforce Participation

Prompt, meaningful feedback—both automated and personal—is essential for validating newcomers' efforts. Automated responses, like "thank you for your first post" notifications, offer immediate acknowledgment, reducing uncertainty about reception and norms.

More impactful are personalized feedback instances, where mentors or community leaders respond with encouragement or constructive input. Such interactions communicate that newcomers are seen and their contributions matter, strengthening motivation.

Some communities employ analytics-driven feedback to highlight milestones or suggest next actions, blending technology with human warmth. These feedback loops nurture a positive cycle of participation and belonging.

Measuring Retention and Growth Through Key Metrics

Quantifying the success of recruitment and onboarding informs continual refinement. Common retention metrics include return rate (how many members come back after joining), time to first post (a proxy for activation), and cohort analysis (tracking groups based on their join date to identify patterns).

By monitoring these measures, communities can identify drop-off points in the newcomer journey and test targeted interventions. For example, a sudden decline in activity after sign-up may signal onboarding gaps, prompting revisions to orientation materials or welcome approaches.

Data-driven insights also help balance scale and quality—ensuring rapid growth does not compromise the supportive atmosphere that retains loyal members.

Recruiting and welcoming new members is a nuanced dance of understanding, inviting, guiding, and supporting. Communities that excel do so by treating newcomers not as passive data points but as evolving participants whose early experiences profoundly influence long-term engagement. Thoughtful strategies—grounded in empathy, clarity, and connection—transform first encounters into enduring relationships, laying the groundwork for vibrant, resilient communities.

3.4 Communication Tools and Technologies

At its core, communication is the lifeblood of human connection, and technology has dramatically expanded the channels through which we interact, share ideas, and collaborate. Today's platforms are diverse and ever-evolving, designed to address the nuances of different interaction styles and needs. To understand this landscape, it is useful to differentiate between two fundamental modes: synchronous and asynchronous communication.

Synchronous communication occurs in real time, where participants share a moment simultaneously—think of a face-to-face conversation, only now often mediated by digital tools. In contrast, asynchronous communication unfolds over time, allowing individuals to respond at their convenience, much like exchanging letters across days or weeks. Each mode carries distinct affordances and limitations, shaping how we engage and collaborate.

Synchronous Communication

Real-time interaction has long been prized for its immediacy and fluidity. Early internet chat rooms, emerging in the 1980s and 1990s, pioneered digital synchronous spaces where users could type messages instantly visible to all participants. Today's real-time tools have expanded in sophistication and scope. Instant text-based chat rooms have evolved into organized channels within platforms like Slack or Microsoft Teams, where participants can debate ideas, troubleshoot problems, or simply socialize. These spaces often employ threading: branching conversations within channels that keep discussions coherent and accessible despite the rapid flow of messages.

Voice channels add another layer of immediacy and expression, providing tonal nuance and reducing misunderstandings common in text. Platforms such as Discord or Clubhouse break down barriers between casual hangouts and structured meetings by offering dedicated audio rooms. Here, participants can chime in spontaneously or raise a hand to speak, mirroring the dynamics of an in-person gathering. The rise of webinars and livestreams extends this further into broadcast territory, enabling experts to share insights live with global audiences while allowing for question-and-answer segments that preserve interaction despite the scale.

Video conferencing has perhaps been the most transformative synchronous tool, especially since the global shifts prompted by the COVID-19 pandemic. Services like Zoom, Google Meet, and Microsoft Teams replicate the visual cues and social presence of physical meetings, from facial expressions to shared whiteboards. These platforms often blend text chat and screen sharing, creating a multi-modal environment that supports diverse communication styles and complex collaboration.

Asynchronous Communication

Not all conversations demand the immediacy of real time. Asynchronous communication offers flexibility, letting participants absorb information, reflect, and respond thoughtfully on their own schedules. Email remains a cornerstone of this mode, the digital equivalent of postal mail but vastly faster and more accessible. Despite predictions of its demise, email endures, favored for formal and long-form correspondence.

Forums and message boards extend the capabilities of email by enabling communal discussion threads. Communities built around shared interests—from hobby groups to professional disciplines—utilize forums to archive knowledge, debate topics, and provide support. Issue trackers, often used by software developers, combine elements of forums with task management, allowing teams to document bugs, propose enhancements, and assign responsibilities asynchronously but systematically.

Social feeds, seen in platforms like Twitter, Reddit, or LinkedIn, blend asynchronous sharing with subtle real-time features. Users contribute posts, comments, and reactions that circulate through followers' timelines. While not strictly synchronous, these spaces often experience bursts of rapid interaction around trending topics, blending immediacy with reflective commentary.

Text Chat Platforms

Instant messaging apps sit at the intersection of synchronous and asynchronous communication. The hallmark of these platforms—such as WhatsApp, Telegram, or Signal—is their ability to deliver messages instantly, while also preserving conversations for later reference. Channel organization is paramount: dividing discussions into topics, teams, or interests avoids chaos and facilitates efficient navigation. Threads within chat channels allow users to isolate conversations without fragmenting the broader community, much like sidebars in a group meeting.

Beyond simple text, many chat apps integrate file sharing, emoji reactions, and rich media embedding, creating a lively, multifaceted communication environment. The ease of switching between one-on-one and group chats caters to both deep focus and broad collaboration.

Voice and Video Technologies

Audio rooms and livestreaming extend communication beyond words on a screen to include intonation, pacing, and immediate feedback. Audio-only platforms, gaining traction through apps like Clubhouse or Twitter Spaces, emphasize spontaneity and inclusivity, often allowing listeners to tune in without committing to full participation. This lowers barriers to entry and fosters wide engagement, somewhat democratizing conversations around topics ranging from professional development to casual storytelling.

Webinars combine structured presentation with interactive elements such as polls, chats, and Q&A sessions, balancing broadcast and dialogue. They are especially useful in education, marketing, and training contexts. Livestream integration on social media platforms, from Facebook Live to Twitch, blurs lines between content creation and interactive communication, enabling real-time audience participation through comments and reactions.

Notification Systems

With so many channels and platforms vying for attention, notification systems play a crucial role in managing information flow and engagement. Push notifications alert users to important events, messages, or updates, helping to maintain connection without overwhelming attention. Mentions—in which a participant is tagged directly—serve as precise attention cues, ensuring key collaborators are alerted without disturbing others.

Digest settings offer an antidote to notification fatigue

by aggregating multiple updates into a concise summary delivered at chosen intervals. This balance between urgency and overload is essential for sustained productivity and mental well-being. Customizable notifications empower users to prioritize what matters and reduce distractions.

Integration and Automation

Modern communication platforms rarely exist in isolation; their true power lies in integration capabilities. Application Programming Interfaces (APIs) enable bots and webhooks to automate routine tasks, provide instant responses, or connect disparate services. For example, a bot might notify a team in Slack when new code is uploaded, or a webhook could trigger alerts in a project management tool when a task changes status.

Third-party integrations enrich communication ecosystems by embedding calendars, file storage, analytics, and more directly into conversation spaces. This interoperability reduces friction, centralizes workflows, and promotes seamless collaboration across platforms.

Mobile Versus Desktop Usage

The landscape of communication tools spans devices as much as modalities. Mobile usage dominates personal and informal interactions, prized for ubiquity and convenience. Yet, screen size and interface constraints shape how communication unfolds on smartphones, often favoring brief messages, push notifications, and voice notes.

Desktop environments afford richer interfaces, prioritizing multitasking with large displays, keyboard shortcuts, and integrated toolsets. Professionals engaged in intensive collaboration or complex projects frequently prefer desktop clients or web applications optimized for detail and control.

Cross-platform compatibility ensures users can shift effortlessly between devices, an expectation that communication tools strive to meet. This fluidity supports the modern mobile workforce and the blurred boundaries between work and life.

Accessibility Considerations

Inclusive design in communication tools is not merely ethical but practical, broadening participation and enhancing user experience. Accessibility standards address diverse needs—such as screen reader compatibility, keyboard navigation, color contrast, and captioning for audio and video content.

These features ensure that individuals with visual, auditory, motor, or cognitive impairments can engage fully. Moreover, accessibility often benefits all users by promoting clarity, simplicity, and user-friendly interfaces. As communication technology becomes more embedded in daily life, embracing accessibility is indispensable for equitable connectivity.

Evaluating Communication Tools

Choosing the right communication platform involves a careful balance of factors tailored to context. Scalability is vital for growing communities or organizations, ensuring that tools perform reliably as user numbers increase. Security concerns, including encryption, data privacy, and compliance with regulations, are paramount given the often sensitive nature of shared information.

Cost considerations range from free, ad-supported options to subscription-based enterprise solutions. Beyond price, organizations weigh features, user support, customization, and ease of adoption. Ultimately, the best tools align with users' workflows, cultivate engagement, and foster a culture of open, effective communication.

In the evolving mosaic of human interaction, communication tools and technologies are more than mere conduits—they shape how we collaborate, create meaning, and build relationships. Understanding their diversity, strengths, and constraints empowers us to harness their potential thoughtfully and inclusively.

3.5 Rituals, Events, and Community Culture

At the heart of every thriving community lies a shared culture—a tapestry woven from common practices, values, and norms that guide members' interactions and shape collective identity. This culture is not an abstract notion but a living, breathing ecosystem sustained by ongoing rituals, specially orchestrated events, and symbolic artifacts that embed meaning and foster belonging. Exploring how such recurring practices and distinctive milestones serve as cultural glue reveals the subtle yet powerful ways communities create continuity, affirmation, and cohesion.

Communities, whether virtual or physical, develop through patterns of behavior that signal membership and reinforce shared expectations. Rituals, in this broad sense, are ceremonies or repeated acts performed collectively or individually that punctuate the community's rhythm. These can be as simple as daily check-ins to mark presence, anniversary threads commemorating the community's founding, or "introduce yourself" posts inviting newcomers to weave their stories into the fabric. Each ritual acts as a ritualized moment of acknowledgment—both of self and others—helping members to orient themselves within the group and reaffirm mutual commitment.

Events, often more elaborate and time-limited than rituals, serve complementary functions by energizing and expanding the community. Online events such as Ask Me Anything (AMA) sessions or hackathons provide structured opportunities for engagement, learning, and creativity. Offline counterparts—meetups, conferences, or festivals—offer face-to-face connection, breathing life into virtual bonds and planting seeds for deeper camaraderie. These gatherings are not merely functional; they are performative expressions of community vibrancy, offering shared experiences that become reference points in the collective memory.

Successful rituals and events resonate because they crystallize community values and evoke emotional investment. Consider a popular developer forum where weekly "Show & Tell" threads spotlight members' projects. This ritual does more than share knowledge; it celebrates innovation, fosters pride, and sustains a culture of mutual respect. Similarly, annual anniversary celebrations often rekindle enthusiasm, attract lapsed members back, and mark the community's resilience. These repeated ceremonies forge a temporal continuity that imparts a sense of history and progress, essential for a thriving culture.

Beyond formal rituals and scheduled events, the informal layer of community culture—often called meme culture—acts as a vital social lubricant. Inside jokes, emojis, and recurring motifs create a shared language that signals familiarity and belonging. Such cultural tokens may seem frivolous at first glance, but their recurrent use weaves an intricate web of meanings accessible only to insiders, thus reinforcing community boundaries and identity. For example, a distinctive emoji deployed in a particular chat channel can evoke collective humor, nostalgia, or solidarity, acting as a subtle yet potent form of cultural glue.

Symbolic artifacts like digital badges, roles, or virtual trophies also serve as visible markers of status, achievement, and commitment within the community. These artifacts function similarly to medals or titles in traditional societies—they confer recognition and motivate participation. For instance, a community member who attains a "Top Contributor" badge not only gains acknowledgment but also becomes a role model, signaling pathways to deeper involvement and influence. Such symbolic rewards do more than distinguish individuals; they codify communal values and establish structured hierarchies that sustain orderly interaction.

Storytelling practices are another cornerstone of community culture, embedding identity through narratives that define origin, success, and collective aspirations. Origin myths recount the community's founding vision, framing its trajectory and offering a sense of purpose. Success stories highlight exemplary members whose journeys inspire others, while member spotlights serve to humanize and celebrate diversity within the group. These narrative elements transform abstract values into tangible experiences, making culture palpable and relatable. They also function as informal teaching tools, transmitting norms and motivating newcomers to integrate more fully.

Celebrations and milestones punctuate a community's timeline with moments of shared accomplishment and recognition. Anniversary events, for instance, create opportunities to reflect on growth and challenges while reaffirming commitment. Member recognition programs highlight contributions that uphold community values, boosting morale and deepening loyalty. Achievement showcases—whether for skills, creativity, or service—encourage ongoing engagement by making individual successes communal victories. These moments of collective celebration act as emotional anchors, strengthening bonds and fostering a positive sense of identity.

Behind the scenes, effective event planning is crucial for converting these aspirations into lived experience. Attention to logistics—such as scheduling, venue or platform selection, and technical support—ensures smooth execution. Strategic promotion attracts participation, while clearly assigned hosting roles facilitate welcoming atmospheres and dynamic interaction. Thoughtful post-event follow-up, including feedback collection and sharing highlights, sustains momentum and integrates lessons learned. This organizational craftsmanship transforms moments of potential into genuine cultural milestones.

To preserve and transmit community culture, documentation plays an indispensable role. Wikis, style guides, and archival collections act as repositories of collective knowledge and norms, safeguarding heritage against erosion as membership changes. They allow newcomers to orient quickly, veterans to refresh shared principles, and the community as a whole to reflect on its evolution. Well-maintained documentation anchors cultural continuity, enabling both stability and adaptation in the face of inevitable growth and transformation.

In sum, the interplay of rituals, events, and symbolic artifacts forms the backbone of community culture. Together, they create a dynamic ecosystem where shared meaning, identity, and belonging can flourish. Far from arbitrary traditions, these recurring practices and celebrations are active, purposeful acts of community building—each one a thread binding individuals into an enduring social fabric.

3.6 Sustaining Engagement and Growth

Building a thriving community or platform is only the beginning; sustaining its vibrancy over time requires deliberate strategies, continual measurement, and adaptive management. The challenge lies not merely in attracting users but in keeping them active, connected, and committed as the community evolves. This ongoing process involves understanding engagement metrics, deploying growth strategies, fostering motivation through gamification, and maintaining a healthy cultural and technical environment.

A fundamental step toward sustaining engagement is carefully tracking behavioral indicators. Metrics such as Daily Active Users (DAU) and Monthly Active Users (MAU) provide a baseline understanding of how many members participate regularly versus sporadically. The ratio of DAU to MAU is particularly telling: a high ratio suggests a tightly knit, frequently engaged community, while a low ratio may indicate fleeting or casual involvement. Beyond these, metrics like post frequency and response rates reveal the density and responsiveness of interactions—critical for maintaining a sense of dialogue rather than one-sided broadcasting. Sentiment analysis, often through natural language processing tools, offers insights into the emotional tone of interactions, exposing trends in positivity or conflict that raw activity numbers miss. Together, these measures offer a multi-dimensional view of community health, enabling informed decisions.

Growth, while a natural aspiration, demands nuanced

strategies that respect community quality. Organic growth—driven by member enthusiasm and authentic interest—often produces the most sustainable expansion. Encouraging members to invite peers through referral incentives rewards valuable contributions and fosters trust. Partnerships with complementary platforms or organizations can introduce fresh audiences without compromising community ethos. Content marketing, such as blog posts, newsletters, or webinars, extends reach while enriching members' experience. Importantly, these strategies interlock: growth without sustained engagement risks fleeting membership spikes, while growth driven by genuine value invites deeper involvement.

To nurture that involvement, gamification offers powerful motivational tools. Systems of points, badges, leaderboards, and achievement milestones tap into human desires for recognition, mastery, and competition. For example, awarding badges for answering questions promptly or consistently contributing high-quality posts encourages positive behaviors. Leaderboards stimulate friendly competition, but when designed with care, they enhance inclusion rather than exclusion. Well-crafted achievement systems convert passive viewers into active participants by making engagement rewarding and visible. The key is balance—over-gamification risks trivializing participation or fostering unhealthy rivalries, while under-gamification may leave potential dynamism untapped.

No community flourishes in isolation from its own feedback. Mechanisms such as surveys and suggestion boxes provide structured avenues for members to voice concerns, propose ideas, and feel heard. Regular retrospectives—periodic reviews with staff or leadership teams—and open forums encourage transparency and collective reflection. These inputs inform iterative improvements and foster a culture of participatory governance, strengthening members' sense of ownership and belonging. Feedback loops also allow communities to pivot before emerging problems become entrenched, preserving long-term health.

Modern platforms increasingly rely on data analytics to maintain oversight. Custom dashboards aggregate key indicators of member activity, content trends, and health signals like churn rates or sentiment fluctuations. Tools may visualize participation by demographic segments, highlight emerging influencers, or flag potential bottlenecks. Armed with analytics, community managers can prioritize interventions, test hypotheses, and validate strategies. These data-driven approaches transform guesswork into strategic insight, ensuring effort aligns with impact.

Segmenting members by activity level, expertise, or interests enables targeted engagement. For instance, affiliate experts might receive invitations to lead discussions or moderate content, while casual members could be nurtured with easy-to-digest tutorials or prompts to join introductory conversations. Such categorization acknowledges that communities are not monoliths; diverse participation styles require differentiated approaches. Segmenting also facilitates personalized communication, which enhances relevance and responsiveness, reinforcing member retention.

However, as communities grow, scalability challenges emerge. Increasing moderation loads demand more personnel or sophisticated automation to maintain civility and content quality. Performance bottlenecks can frustrate users if platforms do not scale technically, eroding user experience. Cultural dilution looms as new members bring diverse values and behaviors, risking fragmentation or loss of the original ethos. Proactive planning, such as decentralized moderation models, scalable infrastructure, and cultural onboarding rituals, help to manage these challenges and preserve community coherence.

Inevitable crises test community resilience and leadership. Spam attacks, interpersonal conflicts, or platform outages can disrupt engagement and trust. Effective crisis management involves clear protocols: rapid response to contain damage, transparent communication with members, and swift restoration of normality. Preparing in advance with well-documented procedures, role assignments, and communication plans reduces panic and confusion. Communities that weather crises openly often emerge stronger, having reinforced their norms and camaraderie.

Understanding the community's lifecycle stage sheds light on appropriate strategies. The initial launch demands energetic outreach and rapid onboarding; growth phases focus on scaling and deepening engagement; maturity calls for refinement and renewal to avoid stagnation; decline may signal the need for reinvention or graceful sunset. Awareness of this cycle helps leaders anticipate changing needs rather than reacting belatedly. For example, mature communities often benefit from reinvigorating content streams or fresh initiatives to spark renewed interest.

Continuous improvement is the lifeblood of long-term success. Iterative practices such as A/B testing different features or approaches provide empirical evidence about what works best. Pilot programs allow experimentation on a small scale before wider rollout, minimizing risk. Governance reviews revisit community rules, leadership structures, and goals to ensure alignment with evolving member expectations and external conditions. Embracing a mindset of adaptability rather than rigidity enables communities to thrive amidst shifting social and technological landscapes.

In essence, sustaining engagement and growth requires a delicate orchestration of measurement, motivation, management, and adaptation. Communities that succeed are those that listen attentively to their members, innovate thoughtfully, and steward their culture and infrastructure with care. This enduring stewardship transforms initial enthusiasm into lasting value, making the community a dynamic, supportive, and evolving space for all who participate.

Chapter 4

Social Dynamics and Relationships Online

This chapter examines the human side of virtual communities: how members form bonds, manage conflict, wield influence, collaborate toward shared goals, and negotiate trust, safety, and identity. We begin with the processes that turn strangers into friends and supporters, then explore the norms and moderation practices that resolve disputes. Next, we analyze leadership and power structures, survey collective action and teamwork, and conclude by looking at the mechanisms that build trust and protect privacy, as well as the paradoxes of online identity and anonymity.

4.1 Forming Friendships and Support Networks

Human beings are inherently social creatures, and the quality of our relationships profoundly shapes both individual wellbeing and the resilience of the communities we inhabit. Social bonds provide emotional sustenance, a sense of belonging, and practical support during times of need. Online environments, far from being isolating voids, offer fertile ground for cultivating these connections—transforming virtual spaces into vibrant hubs of friendship and mutual aid. Understanding how such relationships form and endure online reveals much about the dynamics of human interaction in the digital age.

At the heart of this process lies the distinction between *weak ties* and *strong ties*, concepts first articulated by sociologist Mark Granovetter. Weak ties are the loose, casual acquaintances that bridge different social circles, while strong ties are characterized by frequent interaction and emotional closeness. Online, weak ties often emerge through participation in broad interest groups or comment threads where shared hobbies or topical discussions spark initial contact. These light yet numerous connections diversify our social reach and introduce new perspectives, making them invaluable for informational exchange and discovering opportunities. In contrast, strong ties develop more gradually, nurtured through repeated, meaningful exchanges that deepen trust and commitment. These close friendships or support relationships serve as wellsprings of emotional nourishment and practical aid.

The initial spark that propels strangers into conversation is often rooted in the principle of *homophily*—the natural affinity for those who share similar interests, values, or identities. Online platforms excel at amplifying homophily by enabling users to find communities centered on niche passions, professional fields, or life experiences. Whether through a forum dedicated to rare book collecting or a social media group for new parents, these shared attributes create fertile ground for connection. When people recognize common ground, they feel understood and validated, reducing the social friction that typically accompanies new interactions.

Yet, friendship and support extend beyond similarity; they thrive through the accumulation of *social capital*, a term that captures the benefits individuals derive from their social networks. Two forms of social capital play key roles online: *bonding capital* and *bridging capital*. Bonding capital refers to the close-knit ties that reinforce a group's cohesion—family-like support circles or dedicated friend groups offering empathy and assistance. Bridging capital, in contrast, concerns connections that link diverse social groups, facilitating the flow of new ideas and resources across boundaries. Virtual communities, by bringing together individuals from varied backgrounds who share particular interests or goals, offer rich opportunities for both bonding and bridging. This duality enriches members' experiences and extends their collective resilience.

Trust, the lubricant of any lasting relationship, hinges on the *norm of reciprocity*—a social expectation that favors are exchanged and goodwill is repaid. In online contexts, this norm manifests through mutual exchange of information, advice, and support. For instance, when a novice contributor to a technical forum receives clear, helpful guidance, they often feel compelled to offer assistance when others seek help. Such reciprocal interactions build a positive feedback loop: the more users contribute, the more reputation and goodwill they accumulate, encouraging sustained engagement. Trustworthy relationships thus emerge from a delicate balance of giving and receiving, fostering cooperative dynamics within digital communities.

Beyond reciprocity, several subtle *cues for trust-building* signal reliability and integrity in the absence of face-to-face contact. Reputation systems—such as ratings, badges, or endorsement counts—offer visible markers of a user's past behavior, helping newcomers assess whom they can rely upon. Consistency in online behavior, demonstrated through regular participation and respectful communication, further cements trust.

Endorsements or recommendations from respected members act as social proof, amplifying confidence in potential friends or collaborators. Together, these mechanisms compensate for the lack of physical presence and nonverbal cues, allowing trust to flourish in virtual spaces.

Emotional support—an essential aspect of strong online ties—takes shape through various mechanisms tailored to the digital milieu. Peer mentoring programs often pair experienced members with newcomers, creating structured opportunities for guidance and encouragement. Dedicated threads or channels provide safe havens where users share struggles and receive empathic responses, fostering a sense of community and belonging.   Support circles, whether informal groups on messaging apps or formal online therapy forums, offer ongoing emotional scaffolding that helps individuals cope with challenges such as illness, grief, or social anxiety. These modalities demonstrate how digital networks can replicate and sometimes enhance the supportive functions traditionally associated with face-to-face relationships.

Sustaining these connections over time, however, requires deliberate effort and practical strategies. Regular check-ins—simple gestures like asking how someone is doing or sharing updates—keep communication lines open and show ongoing care. Co-participation in activities, such as collaboratively editing a wiki, gaming together, or engaging in group challenges, reinforces bonds by intertwining shared experiences.   Balancing asynchronous interactions with occasional real-time chats or video calls helps maintain intimacy despite geographical distances. By weaving these practices into online routines, individuals transform ephemeral encounters into enduring relationships.

When comparing *online versus offline friendship*, the differences are often less stark than commonly assumed. While digital friendships may initially lack the sensory richness of face-to-face meetings, they can develop comparable emotional depth through sustained, meaningful interaction. Moreover, online platforms often remove barriers—such as mobility constraints or social anxiety—that hinder offline connection, enabling multicultural and geographically dispersed friendships. Yet, the maintenance of any friendship, online or offline, demands mutual investment and responsiveness; no platform alone guarantees quality or durability.

As more users join and participate, *network effects* magnify the value of these social spaces. Larger communities tend to be more diverse, expanding the range of perspectives, experiences, and resources available. This increasing variety enhances the possibilities for forming both bonding and bridging ties, broadening members' horizons. At the same time, growing membership promotes robust support infrastructure; when one member faces difficulty, the large pool of participants increases the chance of timely assistance. Hence, the success and sustainability of online friendship networks often depend on fostering inclusive growth, balanced participation, and evolving norms that encourage supportive interaction.

Through the interplay of affinity, reciprocity, trust, and shared experiences, online environments have transcended mere communication channels—they have become crucibles for forging meaningful relationships and support networks. These digital bonds enrich individual lives and reinforce social resilience in unprecedented ways, illuminating the enduring human capacity to connect, adapt, and flourish in new terrains.

4.2 Conflict, Moderation, and Etiquette

Every thriving community, whether virtual or physical, navigates the delicate balance between diverse opinions and shared respect. Conflict in groups is as inevitable as breaths in a conversation; diverse minds bump against each other, stirring tension but also innovation. Understanding the origins of disagreement, the unwritten rules of engagement, and the active role of moderation reveals how communities maintain civility amid complexity.

At the heart of constructive interaction is community etiquette—an evolving set of norms that reinforce respect, encourage thoughtful tone, and nurture genuine engagement. These community standards ask members to listen with openness, respond with kindness, and challenge ideas without undermining individuals. Simple courtesies such as refraining from personal attacks, acknowledging alternative viewpoints, and avoiding inflammatory language create an approachable atmosphere. This form of social contract fosters trust, allowing voices to flourish without fear of ridicule or dismissal. The power of etiquette lies less in strict rules and more in cultivating an environment where members instinctively choose collaboration over confrontation.

Despite shared norms, conflict arises routinely, often triggered by a few familiar catalysts. Misunderstandings loom large—nuances lost in translation or assumptions made without context quickly escalate disputes. Cultural clashes add another layer, as diverse backgrounds bring different values, communication styles, and expectations that may inadvertently offend or confuse. Competition—over ideas, status, or scarce resources—can sharpen tensions as members vie for influence or recognition. These elements intertwine in unpredictable ways, making conflict a constant challenge for any collective.

Among the various manifestations of conflict, two disruptive behaviors stand out: flaming and trolling. Flaming is typically impulsive and emotional—an angry outburst sparked by frustration or provocation. It often reveals genuine hurt or disagreement but erupts in harsh, sometimes regrettable language. Trolling, by contrast, is strategic and calculated: a deliberate attempt to provoke and unsettle through posted remarks designed to offend or derail. While flaming stems from the heat of the moment, trolling aims to ignite ongoing tension by feeding off reactions. Recognizing the difference helps communities tailor responses—addressing genuine grievances with empathy, while neutralizing provocations quickly to prevent damage.

Online anonymity and the phenomenon of disinhibition further complicate these dynamics. Shielded by pseudonyms or invisibility, individuals sometimes shed social restraints, feeling less accountable for their words and actions. This reduced accountability can embolden members to express hostility or engage in disrespectful behaviors they might avoid in face-to-face interactions. Such anonymity can simultaneously protect vulnerable voices and amplify negativity, demanding careful consideration in community design. Understanding this double-edged nature is key to crafting environments that balance freedom with responsibility.

To uphold civility, communities rely heavily on moderation—an essential layer of stewardship that guides discourse, enforces norms, and diffuses conflicts. Moderators and administrators act as guardians, balancing impartiality with authority. Their duties encompass monitoring conversations, interpreting and applying rules fairly, and intervening when boundaries are crossed. Beyond rule enforcement, moderators often play a crucial role in fostering inclusion, modeling respectful behavior, and nurturing a sense of belonging. This stewardship requires not only vigilance but also emotional intelligence and diplomacy.

Complementing human oversight are a range of moderation tools designed to streamline management and preempt disorder. Flags allow members to report inappropriate content, triggering review processes that combine automated filters and human judgment. Automated bots scan for spam, offensive language, or repeated rule violations, providing swift initial responses. However, machine intervention cannot replace nuanced evaluation, which is why many communities maintain workflows for manual review to ensure context-sensitive decisions. This blend of technology and human insight optimizes moderation efficiency without sacrificing fairness.

Communities also thrive on self-moderation mechanisms where members collectively uphold civility. Peer policing encourages individuals to gently correct or caution others, reinforcing norms through social bonds rather than authoritarian controls. Reputation systems reward positive contributions with badges, points, or privileges, incentivizing constructive participation and discouraging harmful behavior. These internal motivators tap into human desires for recognition and belonging, transforming members from passive observers into active custodians of community standards.

When conflicts do escalate despite preventive efforts, structured resolution processes become vital. Mediation techniques invite disputing parties to communicate openly under the guidance of a neutral facilitator, focusing on mutual understanding rather than punishment. De-escalation scripts offer scripted language and strategies to cool hot tempers and reframe arguments constructively. Cooling-off periods, where conversations pause before resuming, give participants time to reflect and regain composure, reducing the risk of inflammatory exchanges spiraling out of control. Such processes underscore the community's commitment to reconciliation over retribution.

Should disruptions persist, escalation paths provide graduated sanctions designed to deter future infractions while preserving community health. These may begin with warnings—friendly but firm reminders of standards—escalate to suspensions limiting participation temporarily, and culminate in bans that remove disruptive elements entirely. Well-designed appeals procedures offer transparency and fairness, allowing users to contest decisions and ensuring moderation does not become arbitrary or oppressive. Clear, consistent enforcement strengthens trust in the system and signals that civility is a shared responsibility.

Maintaining civility is an ongoing endeavor—one reinforced by recurring reminders of community values, leaders who exemplify ideal behavior, and restorative practices that mend relationships. Regularly revisiting norms helps keep standards fresh in members' minds, especially as communities evolve or grow. When prominent figures model empathy and respect, their influence cascades through the group, setting a powerful example. Restorative approaches address harm by encouraging offenders to acknowledge impact and make amends, transforming conflict into opportunity for growth and stronger connection.

Together, these elements form a mosaic illustrating how

communities negotiate discord and foster harmony. Conflict is not the enemy, but rather a catalyst for refinement when approached with intention and care. Through a combination of etiquette, moderation, and shared responsibility, communities create resilient spaces where diverse perspectives coexist and enrich collective life. It is this dynamic interplay that transforms potential chaos into collaborative possibility.

4.3   Influence, Leadership, and Power Structures

Leadership, at its core, is about guiding, organizing, and inspiring members within a group or community to achieve common goals. It involves more than just issuing directives; effective leaders shape the environment in which ideas circulate, trust forms, and motivated action unfolds. The essence of leadership lies in navigating the tensions between authority—formal or informal—and the organic momentum that arises among participants.   Understanding how influence and power emerge reveals much about the social architecture of any collective endeavor.

Unlike formal authority, which derives from official appointments or designated positions, leadership can also arise spontaneously among members who gain respect and trust through their contributions and expertise.   Whereas a committee chairperson might be selected to oversee meetings and enforce rules, an informal leader could be a veteran participant who volunteers guidance, shapes norms, or champions innovative ideas without ever claiming a title. This contrast between appointed officials and organically emergent influencers highlights how communities balance structure with flexibility. Formal roles provide clarity and accountability, but grassroots leaders often energize the group by embodying its values and responding dynamically to its needs.

Within many communities, gatekeepers and elders occupy a distinct niche. These veteran members curate content, uphold standards, and act as custodians of tradition. Their authority is less about wielding power overtly and more about maintaining the health and integrity of the collective. They vet contributions, moderate disputes, and pass down unwritten codes that preserve cohesion. Such roles are particularly vital when formal mechanisms alone prove insufficient to address subtle social dynamics or evolving challenges. By selectively amplifying voices and filtering noise, gatekeepers help the community navigate complexity with continuity.

In modern online and organizational contexts, reputation systems serve as quantifiable markers of authority and trustworthiness. Points, badges, and up-votes act as visible tokens signaling participants' expertise, commitment, or popularity. These systems make influence more transparent, assisting newcomers in discerning whom to listen to or collaborate with. Yet reputation remains a currency that communities continuously negotiate; its value depends on the collective's shared interpretation and on evolving contributions. A badge earned years ago may not guarantee relevance today, just as a fresh insight might quickly recalibrate perceptions of authority.

Beyond reputation mechanics, influencer roles diversify the ways individuals impact their networks. Ambassadors often serve as bridges between groups, extending reach and fostering alliances. Thought-leaders stimulate discourse, challenging orthodoxies and suggesting new paradigms. Meanwhile, micro-influencers operate within niche circles, wielding deep but focused sway over specialized interests. Together, these varied roles form a constellation of influence that adapts fluidly to shifting contexts. Influence is rarely monopolized; instead, it diffuses across multiple nodes, each amplifying different facets of communal life.

Social proof—the psychological phenomenon where people imitate the choices of others—plays a pivotal role in steering participation and shaping consensus. Endorsements, trending content, and visibly popular opinions attract additional attention, often producing cascades of agreement or engagement. This dynamic can accelerate decision-making and coordination but also risks reinforcing existing biases or marginalizing minority perspectives. The dance between social validation and independent judgment determines whether a community embraces diversity or converges prematurely on dominant narratives.

A useful dimension of power structures lies in examining centralized versus distributed authority. Centralized power concentrates decision-making in a few hands, enabling swift action and clear accountability. Distributed power spreads authority broadly, fostering participation, resilience, and shared ownership. Each model has merits and pitfalls: centralized systems may become rigid or authoritarian, while distributed systems can struggle with coordination and decisiveness. Hybrid arrangements often emerge, blending top-down control with collective deliberation to balance efficiency and inclusiveness.

Within these frameworks, the *spiral of silence* illustrates a subtle but profound social dynamic: when individuals perceive their views as minority opinions, they may hesitate to express dissent, fearing isolation or reprisal.

106

This silence reinforces the apparent dominance of majority views, sometimes obscuring the true diversity of thought. Recognizing this effect is crucial for cultivating environments where alternative perspectives can surface and dialogue remains vibrant. Without intentional encouragement of dissent, communities risk homogeneity and stagnation.

Nurturing leadership thus becomes an ongoing practice rather than a fixed arrangement. Mentoring new leaders, rotating responsibilities, and providing opportunities for skill development ensure leadership remains dynamic and responsive. Such practices democratize influence, prevent burnout among incumbents, and replenish the pool of trusted guides. Leadership development fosters a culture where authority is earned and earned anew, rather than simply inherited or imposed.

Balancing power requires institutionalized safeguards that check potential abuses and uphold fairness. Appeal boards, grievance processes, and governance charters function as essential counterweights to prevent concentration of power and arbitrariness. These mechanisms embody transparency and accountability, reassuring members that authority is exercised responsibly and subject to review. Effective power balances create trust that the system serves collective interests rather than individual agendas.

Together, these facets sketch a nuanced landscape where influence and power are neither fixed nor absolute. Leadership emerges along fluid fault lines between formal appointment and informal respect, between centralized command and distributed agency. It is shaped by social cues such as reputation and endorsement, sustained by traditions stewarded by gatekeepers and elders, and energized by networks of influencers who amplify ideas across boundaries. The interplay of these forces determines not only who leads, but how leadership transforms communities, enabling them to evolve, adapt, and thrive.

4.4   Collaboration   and   Collective Action

At its core, collaboration is the art of working together, and collective action refers to the joint efforts of a group to achieve goals that would be difficult or impossible for any individual to accomplish alone. In the digital realm, collaboration and collective problem-solving take on new dimensions, allowing dispersed communities to pool diverse talents, knowledge, and resources through online platforms. This coordinated synergy enables groups to tackle complex challenges—whether composing an encyclopedia, building open-source software, or responding to global crises—by sharing the cognitive load and harnessing a collective brainpower far greater than any solitary mind.

One of the most remarkable phenomena underlying successful collaboration is *collective intelligence*: the emergent property whereby the aggregated expertise and creativity of many outperform what any single expert could manage.   Unlike mere crowds, which might simply amplify noise, genuine collective intelligence forms when participants with heterogeneous backgrounds coordinate thoughtfully, correcting one another's errors and building cumulatively on insights. For instance, consider how Wikipedia's millions of volunteer editors continuously refine articles through iterative improvements—catching inaccuracies and adding nuanced detail—resulting in a living repository of knowledge that rivals traditional encyclopedias in scope and reliability.

Key to enabling such outcomes are *coordination mechanisms* that organize the collective effort. In distributed teams, clearly defined roles help prevent duplication of work and ensure accountability. Task boards become indispensable visual tools, mapping out responsibilities and progress so everyone knows what's done, what's pending, and who's responsible. Well-designed workflows guide the flow of tasks, reviews, and feedback loops, keeping disparate contributors synchronized despite geographical and temporal gaps. For example, open-source projects hosted on platforms like GitHub rely on issue trackers, pull requests, and continuous integration pipelines to coordinate development among hundreds or thousands of programmers.

Yet coordination is only part of the puzzle; *decision-making in groups* often demands explicit structures. Voting mechanisms let collectives gauge majority preferences, but risk marginalizing minorities. Consensus seeks to incorporate all voices, fostering broad commitment but sometimes at the cost of speed. Meritocratic selection—where contributions are weighted by expertise or reputation—attempts to balance inclusivity with quality. Each approach has trade-offs: student government elections rely on voting; scientific collaborations might seek consensus through discussions; and online communities might entrust moderators chosen for their track record to arbitrate disputes. The choice of decision-making method shapes not only efficiency but group cohesion and legitimacy.

Equally vital is *task division*, where large projects are decomposed into modular components assigned according to contributors' strengths or interests. Specialization not only leverages expertise but reduces cognitive overhead, as individuals focus on manageable pieces rather than the entire system. However, more modules mean more interfaces and dependencies, requiring careful integration management to prevent bottlenecks or conflicts. For example, a massive open-source operating system kernel is subdivided into drivers, core scheduling, filesystem code, and user interfaces—each maintained by dedicated teams who regularly synchronize their efforts to maintain overall coherence.

Crowdsourcing models harness these principles by inviting open calls for contributions from the broader public, ranging from problem-solving contests and data annotation to creative content generation. The incentive structures behind crowdsourcing vary widely: some rely on altruism, others offer monetary rewards, reputational benefits, or gamified points to motivate participation. The success of platforms like Foldit— which crowdsources protein folding puzzles to citizen scientists—and Amazon Mechanical Turk reflects how well-designed incentives can mobilize large-scale participation, converting a diffuse crowd into a powerful resource for research, innovation, and development.

At the heart of many collaborative endeavors lie *shared artifacts*—wikis, shared documents, code repositories— that serve as both the medium and memory of collective work. These digital commons are more than static archives; they are dynamic, evolving hubs where knowledge is created, edited, and refined in real time. The openness of access and ease of editing lower barriers to entry and empower newcomers to join ongoing conversations. For instance, collaborative platforms like Google Docs or Wikimedia facilitate asynchronous input, enabling contributors worldwide to converge on a single, ever-improving product.

However, successful collaboration also requires thoughtful *governance of projects* to navigate conflicts, allocate resources, and ensure sustainable growth. Governance structures vary from informal steering committees—groups of trusted contributors who set priorities—to formal working groups focused on specific deliverables, often supported by contributor license agreements that clarify ownership and usage rights. Such frameworks cultivate trust and predictability, striking a delicate balance between centralized leadership and decentralized participation essential for long-term viability. The Linux Foundation's governance model illustrates how collaborative legitimacy and coordinated direction can coexist in a sprawling, volunteer-driven ecosystem.

Motivating participants in collective efforts is a subtle art that transcends simple remuneration. While some contributors are paid professionals, many volunteer their time driven by intrinsic rewards: recognition by peers, the satisfaction of co-authorship, or the thrill of solving open challenges. Gamified systems—leaderboards, badges, or virtual currency—leverage human psychology, turning mundane tasks into engaging pursuits. Open-source contributors often testify that their strongest motivators are community respect and the opportunity to improve software they themselves rely on. Understanding and nurturing these diverse motivations is crucial to sustaining the momentum of collective projects, especially as external incentives fluctuate.

As collaborations scale from small teams to vast communities, the complexity of *scaling collaboration* intensifies dramatically. Early-stage projects might rely on simple chat apps and face-to-face meetings, but large-scale initiatives demand robust tooling and process adaptations to maintain clarity and productivity. Automated workflows, advanced project management

111

software, and standardized conventions help manage
the flood of contributions and communications. Social
norms evolve alongside technical infrastructure to
manage conflicts, onboard newcomers efficiently, and
protect against burnout. For example, Wikipedia's
evolving policies and bots help automatically detect
vandalism, while massive coding projects adopt
continuous integration and modular design to reconcile
thousands of daily changes.

The story of collaboration and collective action is one
of human ingenuity harnessed through connection,
structure, and shared purpose. By dividing labor
intelligently, coordinating decisions democratically, and
nurturing a diverse array of motivations, communities
amplify their collective intelligence to achieve feats far
beyond individual reach. In a world increasingly shaped
by global challenges and unprecedented opportunities,
learning how to collaborate effectively—online and
offline—remains one of our most vital skills.

4.5   Trust, Safety, and Privacy

At the heart of every thriving online community lies
a delicate web of trust, safety, and privacy. These
three pillars form the invisible architecture that allows
members to interact confidently, share openly, and
build meaningful connections across digital spaces.
Without them, communities risk fragmentation, harm,
or worse—a complete collapse of engagement and
goodwill. Understanding how trust is constructed, how
safety is enforced, and how privacy is preserved reveals
much about the social dynamics and technological
frameworks shaping our online lives.

Trust begins with transparency, consistency, and

reputation. Transparency means that the rules, processes, and intentions behind a community's operation are clear and accessible. When members can see how decisions are made, who enforces the rules, and why certain behaviors are rewarded or penalized, uncertainty—and with it suspicion— diminishes. Consistency follows naturally: trust blooms when guidelines are applied fairly and predictably, without favoritism or arbitrariness. Reputation, meanwhile, is the social currency earned through repeated interactions. Members who reliably contribute helpful content, behave respectfully, or provide valuable insights accumulate trust points—often informally, but sometimes codified through platform features. Together, these elements foster confidence that the community operates on a shared understanding, rather than hidden agendas.

Reputation and credibility reinforce this foundation through endorsements, testimonials, and scoring systems. Much like the word-of-mouth recommendations in a local neighborhood, online endorsements—"likes," upvotes, endorsements, or expert badges—signal to others which members or content are dependable. Testimonials serve a similar purpose by publicly recording experiences or feedback that attest to a participant's trustworthiness. Scores or ratings, whether they measure quality, reliability, or friendliness, provide immediate visual cues that help newcomers decide whose content to consume or whom to interact with. These systems transform abstract trust into measurable and communicable forms, layering social proof over personal judgment. Yet they also introduce challenges: inflated or manipulated scores may distort perceptions, requiring careful platform design and user awareness to maintain integrity.

Clear community guidelines are indispensable for defining acceptable behavior and setting boundaries. Like a social contract, these policies articulate what is encouraged, what is tolerated, and what is forbidden. They construct a shared moral and practical framework, making it easier for members to self-regulate and for moderators to intervene. Enforcement is key: guidelines that are ignored or inconsistently applied quickly lose authority, fostering confusion or resentment. Effective frameworks are drafted openly, updated regularly, and paired with education or onboarding efforts to help members understand their purpose.   This transparent codification of norms signals a community's commitment to safety and respect, inviting participation while discouraging harm.

Reporting mechanisms translate the community's values into action by empowering members to flag problematic behavior.   Features such as flagging offensive posts, blocking disruptive users, or escalating severe issues to moderators provide essential tools to address abuse promptly.   These channels offer more than just complaint departments—they shape a community's responsiveness and resilience. Effective reporting systems are user-friendly, protect those who report from retaliation, and follow through with fair investigations.   Without such mechanisms, harmful behavior can fester unchecked, eroding trust and driving away vulnerable members. By contrast, visible responsiveness reassures users that the community cares about their well-being and safety.

Online safety risks are real and multifaceted, from targeted harassment to doxxing, from subtle intimidation to overt hate speech.   Harassment—a sustained campaign of hostile or threatening behavior—can happen in comments, direct messages, or even via external channels. Doxxing, the exposure of private personal information such as home addresses or phone numbers, threatens physical safety and privacy simultaneously. Hate speech fuels divisiveness and marginalization, making spaces unwelcoming or outright dangerous for minority groups. Recognizing the diversity and seriousness of these threats helps communities develop comprehensive strategies that protect members without stifling free expression. Mitigating harm demands vigilance, clear response protocols, and technological support to detect patterns and intervene swiftly.

Platforms themselves implement a variety of safeguards to curb risks and maintain healthy interaction. Content filters screen out profanity, spam, or flagged keywords before they reach users, reducing immediate exposure to harmful or unwanted material. Rate limiting controls how frequently members can post or comment, preventing harassment campaigns or overwhelming floods of content. Age-gating features restrict access according to users' verified age, protecting minors from unsuitable content or interactions. While none of these tools are perfect alone, their combined use creates layered defenses that raise the barrier against abuse and inappropriate behavior. The continual refinement of such safeguards illustrates the ongoing balancing act platforms face between openness and control.

Protecting personal data is an equally crucial dimension of online community design. Encryption ensures that sensitive information—messages, credentials, payment details—is scrambled during transmission and storage, reducing vulnerability to interception or hacking. Anonymization techniques strip identifiable markers from data collections used for research or analytics, preserving user privacy even as the platform learns and

evolves. Compliance with data protection standards
such as the General Data Protection Regulation (GDPR)
or the California Consumer Privacy Act (CCPA) holds
platforms accountable to legal and ethical norms,
mandating transparency, control, and security around
personal information. These measures underpin trust
in how communities handle private details, reassuring
members that participation does not come at the cost of
safety or dignity.

Yet, privacy concerns persist amid the vast appetite for
user data by platforms and third parties. Profiling—
building detailed user personas based on behavior,
preferences, and connections—can lead to intrusive
targeted advertising or algorithmic manipulation.
Tracking users across different sites or devices raises
questions about consent and boundaries, as their
digital trails are aggregated to predict and influence
behavior. Data sharing with external companies adds
further risks, potentially undermining users' control
over who accesses their information. These challenges
invite ongoing scrutiny, demanding transparency, user
agency, and meaningful choices about how personal
data is collected, stored, and used.

Anonymity offers both sanctuary and complication
within this landscape. On one hand, anonymous
participation enables freer self-expression, particularly
for marginalized voices or those discussing sensitive
subjects. It lowers the fear of judgment, social stigma,
or professional repercussions, fostering candor and
diversity. On the other hand, anonymity can weaken
accountability, emboldening trolls, bullies, or malicious
actors who exploit invisibility to disrupt or harm.
Striking the right balance requires nuanced policies—
allowing anonymity where beneficial but combining
it with mechanisms that discourage abuse, such as

reputation systems or verified identities in certain contexts. The debate over anonymity's place in online communities underscores the complexity of human behavior and the perpetual negotiation between freedom and responsibility.

Digital consent forms the ethical backbone that connects trust, privacy, and community engagement. Informed consent means users understand what data they provide, how it will be used, and with whom it might be shared— especially when third-party services integrate into the platform. This transparency empowers users to make deliberate choices rather than unwittingly surrender their information. Consent processes should be clear, accessible, and revisable, avoiding dark patterns that manipulate users into agreement. Moreover, ongoing dialogue about data practices—and opportunities to withdraw consent—reinforce the notion that personal information remains under the individual's control, not the platform's sole prerogative.

Together, these mechanisms create a complex ecosystem in which trust is not a given but an achievement—built up cautiously, maintained vigilantly, and renewed continuously. Online communities that succeed in fostering trust, safeguarding members, and protecting privacy become more than just digital meeting places; they transform into resilient social structures where individuals can truly connect, collaborate, and thrive.

4.6 Identity and Anonymity

In the vast and ever-expanding world of the internet, identity is a complex, multifaceted construct shaped by both technological affordances and social conventions. Unlike face-to-face interactions, where identity cues are rich and immediate, online identity is often a carefully curated assemblage of profiles, bios, avatars, and usernames. These digital signifiers create a sense of presence and personality, yet they also introduce new challenges, as the boundaries between authenticity, anonymity, and accountability blur.

Online identity construction begins with profiles—those concise digital dossiers that blend factual details, expressive statements, and visual markers. A carefully crafted bio may highlight a user's interests, profession, or values, while an avatar—a graphical representation that might be a photo, illustration, or abstract icon—adds an emotional or stylistic dimension. Together, these elements convey not only who users are but also who they aspire to be perceived as. For instance, a scholar might feature a professional headshot and a concise research-focused bio on an academic platform, while the same individual might adopt an anonymous cartoon avatar and playful tagline in a gaming community, signaling a different facet of their identity. The choices embedded in these curated identities allow users to navigate diverse social terrains, communicating membership, status, or mood at a glance.

Visual and textual self-presentation cues operate hand in hand. While avatars provide immediate visual impressions, textual elements—such as personalized usernames, status messages, or stylistic tone—offer subtler insights into personality. Consider how the difference between `johndoe123` and `WittyPenguin` as a handle evokes different expectations: the former suggests formality or perhaps anonymity, the latter whimsy or openness to humor. These cues help form first impressions and influence how others interpret messages and engage in dialogue. Equally important is the platform context, as different environments prompt distinct modes of self-expression. A professional network encourages restraint and polish, while social media or discussion forums invite casualness and experimentation.

This interplay brings us to a crucial tension in online identity systems: the contrast between real-name, authenticated identities and pseudonymous or handle-based systems. Platforms like LinkedIn and Facebook traditionally enforce or encourage real-name use, tying digital interactions closely to offline identity. This fosters a sense of accountability, as users are generally recognizable and can be held responsible for their conduct. On the other hand, pseudonymity—using a consistent but non-real name, sometimes linked to an evolving persona—pervades spaces such as Twitter, Reddit, or online gaming. Here, the handle becomes a kind of brand or signature, offering a mix of recognition and privacy. The benefits of such pseudonyms include freedom to express controversial opinions, experimentation with identity, and protection from harassment or surveillance. Yet, this very freedom also opens avenues for deception, trolling, or evasion of responsibility.

An intriguing aspect of online identity is the proliferation of multiple personas across different communities. Unlike offline social circles, where a single identity is often assumed stable, online users routinely adopt role-based avatars tailored to various contexts. A single individual might be an authoritative expert in a professional forum, a passionate fan in a creative space, and a casual participant in a gaming server. These multiple identities are not mere facades but serve social and psychological purposes—allowing users to manage impressions, explore diverse facets of self, or compartmentalize private versus public lives. The resulting patchwork challenges traditional notions of a singular, coherent self, suggesting instead a fluid, dynamic process of identity performance.

This fluidity also ties into the affordances of anonymity, a foundational characteristic of many digital spaces. Anonymity lowers barriers to participation, enabling those who might otherwise hesitate—due to fear of judgment, social stigma, or retaliation—to join conversations and contribute ideas. It cultivates a degree of risk-taking, encouraging more candid disclosure, political dissent, or creative experimentation. However, this freedom has a double edge. The "online disinhibition effect" describes how anonymity and invisibility can lead to behavior that departs from offline norms, sometimes veering into rudeness, hostility, or harmful acts. Freed from immediate social sanctions, people may reveal taboo thoughts or engage in harassment that they would avoid in face-to-face settings. The challenge is to harness anonymity's liberating potential while mitigating its dark side.

In response, many platforms implement layered identity verification methods to modulate these dynamics. Common techniques like email confirmation, phone number linking, or two-factor authentication add credibility and raise the cost of deception, anchoring accounts more firmly to real individuals. These steps do not necessarily reveal a user's full identity but create a trust infrastructure that helps communities distinguish genuine users from bots or impersonators. Verification mechanisms balance privacy concerns with the practical need for reliability, forming the backbone of efforts to foster safer and more constructive interactions.

Nevertheless, risks persist in the form of "catfishing"— the deliberate creation of false identities to deceive others, often for emotional manipulation, fraud, or social engineering. Similarly, impersonation involves adopting another's persona to damage reputation, sow confusion, or exploit trust. Such abuses undermine community cohesion and frustrate moderation efforts. Strategies to combat these issues involve a combination of technological safeguards, such as biometric cues or metadata analysis, alongside social protocols like peer reporting, community vetting, and transparent moderation policies. Education about digital literacy and critical awareness is equally vital, helping users recognize suspicious behaviors and protect themselves.

Underlying these tensions is the perennial balancing act between privacy and accountability. Members' rights to control personal information and maintain anonymity must be weighed against the community's interest in preventing abuse, harassment, and misinformation. Excessive demands for identity disclosure risk chilling participation, particularly among vulnerable groups or dissidents, while overly lax policies invite disorder and mistrust. The optimal balance depends on the community's values, goals, and risk profile, often requiring nuanced and adaptable frameworks rather than rigid rules.

Such considerations inform best practices for community guidelines that empower users to choose their level of identity disclosure while preserving social order. These policies may allow optional anonymity or pseudonymity, coupled with well-defined norms around acceptable behavior and complaint resolution. Transparency about data use and protection builds trust, incentivizing voluntary verification without coercion. Encouraging users to adopt consistent personas also aids reputation-building, fostering accountability without sacrificing privacy.

In navigating the intricate dance of identity and anonymity, online communities mirror broader social questions of who we are, how we represent ourselves, and what responsibilities attach to those representations. The digital realm offers unprecedented freedom to experiment and connect but demands ongoing reflection and innovation to sustain environments that are both vibrant and respectful. By understanding these dynamics, users and architects of online spaces can better harness the potential of identity's multiplicity, anonymity's protection, and accountability's safeguards—crafting communities that reflect the complexity and richness of human interaction in the 21st century.

Chapter 5

Technology: The Architecture of Community

This chapter examines how platform technology—from user interfaces to back-end security—shapes the experience, growth, and resilience of virtual communities. We start with design principles and interface patterns that guide member interaction, then unpack algorithms and recommendation systems that surface content. Next, we compare device-specific and hybrid experiences, survey the security and moderation tools that protect communities, explore accessibility and inclusive design practices, and conclude with a look at emerging innovations that will define the next generation of online social spaces.

5.1 Platforms and Their Interfaces

At the heart of any digital platform lies its interface—a bridge that connects users to content, tools, and each other. The design of this interface often determines whether users feel welcomed, confident, and empowered, or lost, frustrated, and disengaged. To appreciate how platforms craft these experiences, it is essential to understand the foundational design

principles guiding interface creation: consistency,
feedback, affordances, and simplicity.

Consistency ensures that similar elements behave
and appear the same across a platform. When a
button looks clickable on one page, it should look
clickable everywhere; when a notification pops up,
it should always appear in a familiar location. This
uniformity reduces cognitive load, allowing users to
form mental models and navigate more intuitively.
Complementing consistency, feedback provides users
with clear responses to their actions—whether it is a
subtle animation confirming a button press, a sound
indicating message delivery, or an error message
clarifying a failed upload. These signals reassure users
that the platform is responsive and reliable. Affordances
intuitively communicate possible actions; for example,
a raised button hints at pressing, while a slider invites
dragging. Finally, simplicity advocates for paring down
interfaces to essentials, avoiding clutter that overwhelms
or confuses newcomers.

These principles do more than just make a platform
usable—they shape users' first impressions and ongoing
engagement. The initial moments upon landing on a
site or opening an app are crucial. Clean layouts, clear
calls to action, and inviting visuals create a sense of
welcome and competence. A well-designed interface
supplies users not only the means to navigate but
also the confidence to explore, participate, and return.
Conversely, if buttons are hidden, menus obscured, or
terminology unfamiliar, users may hesitate or abandon
the platform entirely.

Once inside, navigation becomes the user's compass.
Platforms deploy an array of patterns to guide discovery
and maintain orientation. Menus, whether hamburger
icons on mobile or horizontal bars on desktops, offer

entry points to major sections. Tabs break complex content into digestible pieces, enabling users to switch context without losing their place. Breadcrumbs trace users' paths through hierarchical structures, helping them backtrack or understand their current position. These elements work in concert to avoid the digital equivalent of wandering aimlessly in a maze.

Underpinning navigation is content organization—the unseen scaffolding that arranges discussions, media, or data. Hierarchies group content into nested categories: forums divided into topics and subtopics, for instance, channel conversations into manageable streams. Tags cross-link related items, enabling flexible, non-linear exploration across themes. Such structures help balance breadth and depth, supporting both casual browsing and targeted searches. By making content findable and logically grouped, platforms sustain engagement and community vibrancy.

Interaction affordances—buttons, gestures, icons—serve as signposts to possible actions. A plus sign may signal adding new content, while a trash icon implies deletion. On touch devices, swipe gestures allow users to archive emails or navigate photo galleries smoothly. These cues reduce uncertainty about "what comes next," empowering users to act with confidence and efficiency. Careful design here prevents frustration and accidental missteps, which can erode trust.

Customization options further enhance user experience by acknowledging diverse preferences and needs. Allowing users to switch between light and dark themes, adjust font sizes, or reorganize layouts caters to comfort and accessibility. Notification preferences let individuals choose how, when, and what type of alerts they receive, preventing overwhelm or disengagement. Platforms that invite such personalization cultivate deeper attachment, as users craft environments that suit their habits and values.

Beyond customization lies extensibility—the capacity to expand and tailor platform functionality. APIs enable developers to build plugins, integrate bots, or link external services. For instance, a chat platform might allow third-party apps to automate reminders or translate messages on the fly. These extensions can transform static interfaces into dynamic ecosystems, adapting the platform to evolving user demands and innovations. Extensibility bolsters longevity and community creativity, inviting collaboration beyond original design boundaries.

Maintaining a coherent user experience across different devices presents unique challenges. Cross-platform consistency strives to ensure that the essence of navigation, visual style, and interaction persists whether on desktop, tablet, or smartphone. Recognizing the constraints and affordances of varying screen sizes and input methods, designers adapt interfaces thoughtfully. For example, a menu may expand horizontally on a desktop but collapse into a single icon on mobile. Achieving this balance prevents disorientation and reinforces brand identity, regardless of where or how users engage.

Speaking of identity, the visual design and theming of a platform serve as a cultural lens, projecting community values and norms. Color palettes, typography, and iconography do more than decorate; they signal the platform's character and ethos. A professional networking site may favor restrained hues and clean lines, projecting seriousness and trustworthiness. In contrast, a creative collaboration space might employ vibrant colors and playful layouts, encouraging experimentation and openness. Through these choices, platforms cultivate a shared sense of belonging and guide user conduct subtly but powerfully.

126

Underpinning all these elements is the iterative process of usability testing. Platforms rarely get their interface perfect on the first try. By employing A/B testing—comparing different designs with user segments—developers gather empirical insights into what works best. Feedback loops, whether through surveys, analytics, or direct user interviews, provide a pulse on pain points and opportunities. This cycle of testing, learning, and refining ensures interfaces evolve responsively, aligning ever closer with user needs and expectations.

Together, these facets of platform interfaces weave a complex tapestry. They mediate not just access to information but the quality of interaction, the rhythm of engagement, and the formation of community norms. Every button pressed, menu clicked, and setting adjusted carries the imprint of deliberate design choices, refined through experience and insight. Understanding the interplay of interface design, navigation structures, interaction affordances, customization, and identity reveals the subtle craft that shapes our digital lives— turning mere functionality into meaningful connection.

5.2 Algorithms, Feeds, and Discovery

At the heart of every social media platform, news site, and content aggregator lies a powerful engine: the algorithm. These data-driven formulas decide not only what you see but also how you connect with the digital world. Rather than passively presenting information in chronological order, modern digital platforms curate personalized feeds that aim to capture attention and engagement. This curation shapes the flow of information, influences what ideas and trends rise or fade, and subtly guides user behavior. Understanding how these algorithms work—and the choices and trade-offs they embody—is essential to grasp the dynamics of our online experience.

Algorithmic curation refers to the process by which platforms use vast amounts of user data—preferences, interactions, time spent on posts, connections, and more—to tailor content specifically for each individual. Instead of a one-size-fits-all stream, your feed becomes a personalized mosaic, constantly recalculated to reflect what the system predicts you will find most engaging or relevant.

This personalization builds on machine learning: algorithms detect patterns in your previous likes, shares, and clicks, combining these with information about other users showing similar patterns. The intent is to surface content that maximizes both your satisfaction and the platform's goals, such as keeping you browsing longer, fostering deeper connections, or encouraging interaction.

Early social media feeds were simple chronological lists, showing posts in the order they were published. While straightforward and transparent, purely chronological feeds pose problems on platforms where user connections and activity are extensive—important content can easily be drowned out by noise, creating a cluttered experience.

To address this, relevance-ranked feeds emerged. These reorder content based on predicted interest, placing posts likely to engage you near the top regardless of timing. A hybrid model attempts to strike a balance: some content is shown strictly by recency to preserve freshness, while other items are reordered based on affinity or engagement likelihood.

Each model has trade-offs: chronological feeds offer fairness in visibility but can overwhelm users; relevance-ranked feeds improve focus and engagement but risk creating echo chambers by reinforcing existing preferences. The particular mix a platform chooses shapes the user experience and information landscape.

Behind the scenes, several key approaches to filtering help shape your feed:

- **Collaborative filtering** relies on the wisdom of the crowds. By analyzing the preferences of users with similar tastes, it recommends items that these "neighbors" have engaged with but you have not yet encountered. This method is famously used by services like Netflix to suggest movies based on viewing patterns of similar users.

- **Content-based filtering**, in contrast, focuses on the attributes of the items themselves—topics, keywords, style—and matches these to your own historical interests. If you frequently engage with cooking videos, the algorithm identifies new content with similar features.

- Many platforms blend these methods into *hybrid approaches* that balance user similarity and item characteristics to overcome respective weaknesses.

Algorithms assess multiple signals to decide an item's prominence in your feed. Key inputs include:

- *Engagement metrics*: likes, comments, shares, dwell time, and click-through rates suggest content's popularity and quality.

- *Recency*: newer posts are generally prioritized to keep content fresh.

- *User preferences*: past interactions, explicitly expressed interests, and connection strength influence weighting.

- *Contextual signals*: device type, location, time of day, and trending topics may affect ranking.

The precise formula remains proprietary and adaptive, but it is clear that these signals are combined in complex ways to maximize relevance and the platform's objectives.

A perennial challenge is the *cold start problem*: how to recommend content to new users with little or no interaction history, or how to promote new content with limited engagement signals. Lacking a data footprint, algorithms struggle to personalize effectively.

Platforms mitigate this by employing default popular items, curated lists, or soliciting user preferences during onboarding. They may also rely more heavily on content-based attributes and social connections early on, gradually switching to more personalized collaborative signals as data accumulates. Creative solutions often blend human editorial oversight with algorithmic seeding until the system "warms up."

Feeds are only one avenue for content exposure. Discovery tools play a complementary role, helping users explore new topics, communities, and ideas outside their immediate network or interests. Notable mechanisms include:

- *Search functionality*, allowing direct queries for content or profiles.

- *Trending lists and curated sections*, highlighting currently popular or culturally relevant material.

- *Hashtags and topic tags*, which group content thematically and enable exploration around shared interests.

- *New member or "people you may know" recommendations*, encouraging network growth and serendipitous connections.

These discovery tools often mix algorithmic suggestions with editorial curation, enriching the ecosystem and preventing stagnation.

Algorithms are not static; they continuously refine themselves based on user feedback embedded in everyday actions. Every like, share, comment, or even the choice to scroll past a post sends signals that reinforce or adjust the model's assumptions about your preferences.

This creates a dynamic feedback loop: the feed influences what you see and engage with, and your engagement further informs the feed. Over time, this loop can sharpen personalization, but it also risks narrowing exposure if unchecked.

While personalization improves relevance, it carries risks. Algorithms can inadvertently create *echo chambers*, where users are exposed primarily to views matching their own, or *filter bubbles*, narrowing the perspective and diversity of content encountered.

These effects arise because algorithms optimize engagement—often stronger with emotionally charged or familiar content—rather than balanced information. Moreover, biases can reflect and amplify societal inequalities or stereotypes, suppressing marginalized voices or controversial topics.

Recognizing these pitfalls has prompted debates about the responsibility of platforms to design algorithms that foster diversity and fairness without sacrificing user satisfaction.

To address concerns about hidden algorithmic influences, some platforms have introduced increased transparency and user controls. These may include:

- *Explanations* about why certain content is recommended.

- *Options* to switch from relevance-ranked to chronological feeds.

- *Settings* to adjust interests, mute topics, or block sources.

- *Opt-out choices* that allow users to see unfiltered timelines.

Such tools aim to restore a sense of agency and trust, though their effectiveness depends on accessibility and user awareness.

Finally, the algorithms shaping digital content raise profound ethical questions. They collect and analyze vast personal data, often beyond explicit consent, threatening privacy. The power to shape public discourse creates opportunities for manipulation—whether through misinformation amplification, political bias, or commercial exploitation.

Platforms must balance innovation with accountability, ensuring transparency, safeguarding data, and preventing harm. Ethical algorithm design calls for multidisciplinary collaboration among technologists, ethicists, regulators, and users themselves.

The interplay of algorithms, feeds, and discovery mechanisms forms the backbone of our online engagement.

Invisible yet profound, these systems shape the information landscape, influence our worldview, and mediate our social connections. As users, recognizing their workings helps us navigate more thoughtfully, while as a society, it challenges us to demand designs that prioritize fairness, diversity, and trust.

5.3 Mobile, Desktop, and Hybrid Experiences

From the dim glow of a pocket-sized smartphone to the sprawling canvas of a desktop monitor, our digital experiences unfold across a kaleidoscope of devices. Each form factor—mobile, desktop, or somewhere in between—shapes how we interact, what we can access, and which features come to life. Appreciating these differences is key to designing technology that feels intuitive, seamless, and empowering, no matter the device in hand.

At the heart of this variation lies *device constraints*. Mobile screens typically range from 4 to 7 inches diagonally, offering a tight yet vibrant stage for apps and websites. Desktop displays, by contrast, span from 13 to 30 inches or more, providing ample real estate for complex layouts and dense information. This divergence in screen size directs how content is organized and presented. Input modalities add another twist: on mobiles, touchscreens reign supreme, inviting swipes, taps, and pinches; desktops lean on keyboards and mice, allowing precise clicking and fast typing. Resource availability also varies. Mobile devices generally wrestle with limited processor power, battery life, and memory, while desktops boast heftier capacities, enabling heavier computations and multitasking. This trinity of constraints—screen, input,

133

and resources—forces designers to tailor experiences sensitively. An interface that dazzles on a desktop might overwhelm a mobile screen, while an elegant mobile app may feel sparse or sluggish on a more powerful computer.

Responsive design is the web's elegant answer to this kaleidoscopic environment. Using CSS techniques such as media queries, flexible grids, and fluid images, designers craft layouts that adapt gracefully to different screen sizes and orientations. For instance, a multi-column desktop webpage can gracefully fold into a single, scrollable column on a phone, ensuring readability and usability without sacrificing content. Flexible units like percentages or viewport width let elements scale naturally, while CSS features such as flexbox and grid enable dynamic alignment and spacing. Responsive typography adjusts font sizes to balance legibility with space economy, helping text stay crisp on screens both large and small. This approach reframes web content as fluid and contextually aware, rather than fixed and rigid, knitting together diverse devices into a harmonious visual tapestry.

Yet adapting layout is only part of the story; performance optimization plays a starring role in smoothing these experiences. Mobile networks can be flaky or slow, and smaller devices often lack desktop-class CPU muscle. Techniques such as lazy loading defer the loading of offscreen images or content until needed, shaving precious seconds off initial load time. Resource bundling combines scripts and stylesheets to reduce the number of HTTP requests, speeding page rendering. Network-aware strategies detect connection speed, lowering image resolutions or postponing non-essential downloads when bandwidth is constrained. This vigilant streamlining is critical on mobile, where impatient users and finite data plans demand swift, lean interactions. Even on desktops, trimming fat expedites workflows and conserves energy, proving that performance matters universally.

Native applications, particularly on mobile, harness device capabilities to deliver experiences beyond what the web can easily replicate. Push notifications keep users informed in real time, gently nudging them back into an app with timely updates or alerts. Offline caching preserves functionality when signal drops, enabling note-taking, reading, or editing without interruption. Hardware integration reaches into sensors and peripherals: cameras, GPS, accelerometers, fingerprint scanners, even haptic feedback motors, allowing apps to respond to motion, location, and biometric identity in ways inaccessible to standard web pages. Many users prize such responsiveness and personalization, which feel tailored and robust. However, native development often requires building separate apps for different platforms or maintaining complex codebases.

Web applications, especially Progressive Web Apps (PWAs), strike a compelling balance here. PWAs run in browsers but behave like native apps in many ways: they can be installed to home screens, operate offline with cached assets, send push notifications, and even work across operating systems. This cross-platform reach simplifies deployment and maintenance, as developers manage a single codebase serving multiple device types. Rapid iteration and updates become frictionless, circumventing app store approval delays. While PWAs may not yet match native apps in leveraging every hardware feature, their growing capabilities and accessibility make them a mighty tool for inclusive, scalable digital experiences.

The modern user rarely stays tethered to a single device. Synchronization underpins a fluid digital life where work, play, and communication flow across smartphones, tablets, and desktops seamlessly. Real-time data sync ensures that changes made on one device—like editing a document or marking an email read—appear immediately on another. State preservation remembers where users left off, so reading a book on a phone continues flawlessly on a laptop. Multi-device continuity fosters user satisfaction and productivity, dissolving friction and cognitive load. Services often achieve this through cloud-based backends, managing data consistency and conflict resolution invisibly. When done well, synchronization reframes multiple devices not as isolated silos but as an interconnected ecosystem serving the user's needs.

Context awareness elevates device interactions by tuning features to environment and circumstance. Smartphones excel here, using location services to offer navigation, weather updates, or local deals. Adaptive notifications might calibrate urgency based on user activity or time of day, avoiding undue interruptions. Contextual UI shifts presentation depending on how the device is held, whether in bright sunlight or low light, or if ambient noise demands quieter alerts. Desktops, while less mobile, can leverage other sensors—such as webcams for presence detection or microphones for voice commands—to create richer interactions. Context-aware design transforms devices from mere tools into intuitive companions attuned to the user's momentary situation.

Accessibility, a foundational but often overlooked consideration, must shine consistently across device boundaries. Whether on a tiny mobile screen or a sprawling desktop, controls need clarity: buttons large enough to touch, fonts legible without zooming, color contrasts supporting users with visual impairments. Keyboard navigation and screen reader support must be preserved, especially on desktops where traditional input methods prevail, but also accounted for on mobile devices that may use touch exploration or voice commands. Accessibility is not an afterthought but a design ethic that ensures digital technology serves everyone equitably, embracing diversity of ability and preference.

Security considerations differ notably across platforms. Mobile operating systems typically sandbox apps rigorously, limiting access to system resources and user data to reduce risk. Permission models empower users to control what apps may access—camera, contacts, location—before granting entry. Desktops tend to offer more open file access and background capabilities but also require vigilant antivirus and firewall protections. Data storage approaches vary: mobile apps often encrypt sensitive information locally and in transit, while web apps rely on secure communication protocols and controlled storage mechanisms like IndexedDB or cookies. Each environment presents tradeoffs between flexibility and protection, shaping how developers safeguard users without impeding usability.

Finally, offline functionality remains a litmus test for resilience across device types. Native mobile apps can bundle substantial assets locally, enabling users to interact even in airplane mode or remote areas—writing notes, playing games, consulting cached data. Web apps, leveraging service workers, have grown adept at caching essential resources and recent content, though usually with more limited offline interactivity. Some complex features, such as synchronization or server-dependent computations, naturally require connectivity, but thoughtful design still strives to provide meaningful offline experiences rather than mere "disconnected" error screens. Robust offline support amplifies user confidence that digital access won't be abruptly severed.

Together, these aspects weave the rich tapestry of mobile, desktop, and hybrid digital experiences. Designers and developers who navigate device constraints skillfully, embrace adaptive layouts, optimize performance, leverage native and web strengths, synchronize seamlessly, anticipate context, champion accessibility, uphold security, and support offline use craft technology that transcends boundaries. The ultimate triumph is an experience tailored not only to a device's shape and capabilities but to the rhythms and realities of human life itself.

5.4 Security and Moderation Tools

In the digital age, online communities are as vibrant and diverse as any physical gathering place, yet they face unique perils: bad actors seeking to disrupt interactions, steal information, or exploit vulnerabilities. To sustain safe, welcoming environments, platforms deploy an intricate arsenal of security and moderation tools. These extend beyond mere technical gimmicks; they are the guardians of trust and civility, blending cutting-edge technology with thoughtful design and human oversight.

At the foundation lies *authentication*, the gatekeeper ensuring that users truly are who they claim to be. Early on, simple password policies prevailed—minimally requiring a mix of letters and numbers to thwart guesswork. However, as breaches grew rampant, these basic measures proved insufficient. Today's systems commonly integrate the OAuth standard, which empowers users to log in via trusted third-party services like Google or Facebook. This delegation streamlines access and reduces password fatigue, while also leveraging the robust security infrastructures of these providers.

Single sign-on (SSO) takes this a step further by letting users authenticate once to gain access to multiple interconnected services, enhancing both security and convenience. Complementing these mechanisms is two-factor authentication (2FA), which adds another lock on the door by requiring a second form of verification—often a short-lived code sent to a phone or generated by an app. This measure dramatically reduces the risk of unauthorized access, even if passwords are compromised.

Security extends beyond login credentials into the realm of *privacy by design*—a principle that embeds privacy considerations into the very architecture of digital systems rather than treating them as retrofitted features. This approach emerged as a response to repeated privacy scandals and growing regulatory pressure, insisting that platforms anticipate and mitigate privacy risks from the outset. By limiting data collection, ensuring transparency, and building user control mechanisms into workflows, privacy by design helps protect individual autonomy without stifling innovation.

Central to privacy and security efforts is *data encryption*, the transformation of readable information into coded formats impervious to casual interception. TLS (Transport Layer Security), the invisible force behind HTTPS websites, establishes encrypted tunnels between your browser and the server, safeguarding data in transit from prying eyes. But security doesn't stop there. End-to-end encryption ensures that only the communicating users—not even the service providers—

139

can read messages, a crucial feature in secure messaging
apps. Likewise, encryption at rest protects stored files
and databases, reducing the damage caused if servers
are compromised. These layered protections create a
robust defense posture, guarding sensitive data at every
stage.

However, not all threats come from passive eaves-
dropping. *Spam and abuse* pose relentless challenges,
often overwhelming communities with unwanted or
harmful content. Automated filters assess incoming
posts and messages using heuristics—rules derived
from expert knowledge—and increasingly sophisticated
machine learning classifiers trained to spot patterns of
spam, scams, or harassment. These systems evolve by
learning from vast datasets, making them more adept
at distinguishing genuine content from abuse. Yet, their
decisions are never infallible, which underscores the
importance of continuous tuning and human oversight.

To complement automated detection, *user reporting interfaces* empower community members to flag inappropriate or harmful behaviors. These interfaces often allow for blocking disruptive users and submitting feedback that informs the platform's moderation policies. By
integrating these participatory tools, platforms crowd-
source vigilance and foster a sense of shared responsibility, turning passive users into active custodians of community health.

Taking automation a step further, *moderation bots*
patrol digital spaces, scanning for content that violates
standards. They don't just flag suspicious posts; many
issue warnings or even remove harmful comments
outright, acting as first responders to emerging threats.
While bots operate tirelessly at scale, their rigid
rules occasionally misfire, highlighting the continued
necessity for human intervention.

This leads naturally to *human review workflows,* where trained moderators receive flagged content through managed queues. Sophisticated dashboards present context, user history, and relevant policies, aiding swift and informed decisions. Escalation protocols ensure that complex cases reach senior staff or specialized teams. This human touch is critical, balancing fairness, nuance, and cultural sensitivities in ways that machines cannot replicate.

A further line of defense is *rate limiting and throttling,* techniques that restrict the speed and volume of user actions to defend against brute-force attacks and API abuse. By imposing caps—such as limiting login attempts or message sends per minute—platforms blunt automated attempts to infiltrate accounts or spam communities. These controls act invisibly but effectively, preserving stability without inconveniencing typical users.

Accountability is a cornerstone of trust, which brings us to *audit logs and forensics.* Detailed, tamper-resistant records chronicle user activities, administrative actions, and system events. These logs enable post-incident investigations, helping platforms understand breaches, abuse patterns, or policy violations. They also provide transparency, supporting internal reviews and, when necessary, external compliance audits—an essential element in upholding community standards and legal obligations.

Lastly, the ever-shifting landscape of data protection regulation has propelled platforms toward strict *compliance and standards.* Laws such as the European Union's GDPR and California's CCPA mandate transparency in data handling, limit excessive data retention, and give users rights over their personal information. Adhering to these frameworks demands

constant vigilance and adaptation but ultimately
promotes user trust and platform legitimacy. Industry
best practices—such as regular security audits, data
minimization, and breach notifications—serve both legal
requirements and the moral imperative to safeguard
digital communities.

Together, these layers—authentication, encryption,
automated detection, human review, and regulatory
adherence—form a dynamic ecosystem of defense
and stewardship. Their combined effect is a digital
environment where users can connect, create, and
collaborate with confidence, knowing that their rights
and experiences are actively guarded. As threats
evolve and communities grow, these tools will continue
to adapt, reflecting the ongoing quest to harmonize
openness with safety in the interconnected world.

5.5   Accessibility and Inclusive Design

Virtual communities thrive when they welcome everyone, regardless of ability, background, or circumstance.
Designing these spaces with accessibility and inclusivity
at their core is not just good ethics—it is an essential
practice that transforms digital interactions from barriers into bridges. This means crafting environments that
can be navigated and understood by a diverse range of
users, including those with visual, auditory, cognitive,
or motor impairments, as well as those who speak different languages or come from varied cultural contexts.

Central to accessible design are the *WCAG Principles*,
formulated by the World Wide Web Consortium (W3C),
which offer a clear framework to ensure usability.
These principles are often summarized as perceivable,
operable, understandable, and robust. *Perceivable* means

users must be able to perceive content through sight, sound, or other senses; for example, images should have descriptive text for those using screen readers. *Operable* ensures all functionality is available via different input methods, not just a mouse. *Understandable* emphasizes clarity in how content and controls behave, helping users predict what will happen next. Finally, *robust* means content should be compatible with current and future technologies, such as new assistive devices or updated browsers, ensuring longevity and ongoing accessibility. These principles provide designers and developers a compass that guides choices and balances technical innovation with human-centered needs.

Reducing cognitive load plays a crucial role in making virtual communities welcoming to everyone. Using clear, straightforward language avoids alienating those with learning disabilities or non-native speakers. Consistent layouts help users form mental maps of navigation paths—imagine a website where all menus, buttons, and links change location on every page; confusion grows quickly. Progressive disclosure, the technique of revealing only necessary information upfront and offering more details upon request, prevents overwhelming users with excessive data or options. This approach not only respects diverse cognitive processing speeds but also streamlines the experience for all participants, making digital spaces feel more intuitive and less frantic.

Visual design elements like color contrast and typography also underpin accessibility. Sufficient contrast between text and backgrounds ensures individuals with visual impairments or color blindness can read content without strain. A palette that avoids problematic color combinations—such as red-green pairings—further benefits usability. Typography that prioritizes legibility, including ample spacing between letters and lines, and the use of scalable or responsive fonts, allows users to adjust text size comfortably without breaking layouts. Collectively, these practices embrace the diversity of human vision and create a comfortable reading environment, which is foundational to sustained user engagement.

For many, keyboard navigation is the lifeline for accessing digital content without a mouse. Thoughtful focus management guides users from element to element in a logical order, while *skip links* let them bypass repetitive menus and jump directly to the main content, saving time and frustration. To further enrich this experience, ARIA (Accessible Rich Internet Applications) roles provide semantic meaning to dynamic user interface elements, enabling screen readers and other assistive tools to interpret interactive components correctly. These techniques ensure that virtual communities remain fully interactive and navigable, regardless of the input device a user relies on.

Supporting screen readers involves more than just adding alt text to images; it requires using semantic markup—proper structure through headers, lists, and landmarks—to convey the organization and hierarchy of content. Clear and concise alternative text ensures imagery delivers its intended message. Live region announcements provide real-time updates for dynamic content, such as chat messages or notifications, so users do not miss critical interactions. In virtual communities, these features foster equal participation, allowing those who rely on auditory information to engage as fully as possible.

Assistive technologies extend accessibility by catering to a variety of user needs. Text-to-speech software reads content aloud, benefiting individuals with low vision or reading difficulties. Voice control allows hands-free navigation and interaction, giving agency to those with limited motor functions. Switch devices enable users to control interfaces with specialized hardware customized to their movements or preferences. Designing virtual communities that anticipate and integrate smoothly with these technologies means users encounter fewer barriers and can tailor their experience to what works best for them.

Language and localization broaden inclusivity by acknowledging the multilingual nature of global communities. Offering user interfaces in multiple languages, supporting translation workflows, and respecting locale-specific formats for dates, times, and numbers create richer, more welcoming experiences. Careful localization goes beyond literal translation; it also adapts cultural references and idioms to resonate authentically with target audiences. This attention to detail not only bridges language divides but also affirms cultural identities, promoting a genuine sense of belonging.

The real test of accessibility lies in continuous user testing and feedback, especially involving individuals who use assistive technologies daily. Participatory design invites these users to be co-creators, uncovering hidden usability gaps and generating solutions grounded in lived experience rather than assumptions. Beta testing programs that prioritize accessibility feedback become powerful tools for iteration, improving community tools systematically. By listening to the voices quieted by traditional design processes, virtual spaces become more responsive and adaptable.

Ongoing accessibility monitoring ensures that communities uphold standards as they evolve. Automated audits scan for common issues such as missing alt text or improper color contrast, offering quick insights for developers. Manual reviews catch subtler problems that technology may overlook, such as ambiguous language or inconsistent navigation cues. Generating compliance reports not only provides transparency but also fuels organizational accountability, making accessibility an integral part of the development lifecycle rather than a one-time checklist.

Beyond technical measures, inclusive community policies weave accessibility into the social fabric of virtual spaces. Guidelines encouraging respectful and inclusive language, options for personal pronouns, and provision of captions or transcripts for multimedia content reinforce that inclusion is both a technical and a cultural commitment. By attending to how people express identity and communicate, virtual communities send a powerful message: everyone belongs here, in all their complexity.

Taken together, these design practices and standards form a layered defense against exclusion. Accessibility and inclusive design are not afterthoughts or burdensome requirements—they are the foundation of virtual communities that welcome all voices and experiences. As digital spaces continue to grow into vital arenas for connection, dialogue, and creativity, fostering accessibility ensures that no one is left on the margins of the online world.

5.6 Innovations and Future Technologies

The contours of community formation, interaction, and governance are undergoing a profound transformation, driven by a tide of emerging technologies. These innovations promise not only to expand the scale and immediacy of human connection but also to challenge longstanding assumptions about how communities function and flourish. To apprehend this unfolding landscape, one must examine the distinct yet interwoven advances in artificial intelligence, immersive realities, decentralized systems, and more, each shaping the social fabric in novel and often surprising ways.

Artificial intelligence (AI) sits at the forefront, reimagining the very architecture of online communities. Gone are the days when moderation was solely a human burden or content creation a static endeavor. Today, AI systems analyze vast streams of text, images, and video in real time, enabling smarter moderation by flagging inappropriate behavior swiftly and consistently. Rather than banning entire groups or silencing participants excessively, AI-driven tools customize responses to context, often providing warnings or fostering dialogue to de-escalate tensions. Moreover, AI fuels new forms of content generation: from automatically crafting summaries and personalized news feeds to producing evocative artwork or music tailored to communal tastes. This personalized experience deepens engagement by interlacing individual preferences with collective narratives, subtly guiding members toward shared understanding without overt intrusion.

Parallel to AI's cognitive revolution is the rise of virtual and augmented reality (VR/AR), technologies that transcend conventional screen-based interfaces. Immersive environments enable communities to coalesce in three-dimensional spaces where physical distance dissolves into curated experiences. Picture a group of collaborators meeting around a virtual campfire, their avatars sharing gestures and emotions as if face-to-face, or a concert taking place on a

147

spectacled augmented landscape overlaying one's physical surroundings. VR and AR reanimate social interaction by providing embodied presence—users experience community not as disembodied text on a screen but as spatially situated participants in dynamic worlds. These avatar-based social spaces invite new rituals and norms, reshaping how trust, identity, and empathy develop among members.

Voice and conversational interfaces further enrich this evolving ecosystem by adding fluid, natural modes of communication. Chatbots and voice assistants now serve as approachable guides, answer questions, and mediate conflicts, effectively acting as community facilitators with infinite patience. Their capacity to understand context and sentiment is maturing, allowing conversational UIs to offer personalized support that adapts to a member's mood or needs. In communities spanning different languages or abilities, these tools break down barriers, fostering inclusiveness through speech recognition, translation, and accessibility features. Rather than replacing human conversation, they augment it—offering on-demand assistance and ensuring no participant is left unheard.

Underlying these user-facing innovations are radical shifts in infrastructure, most notably decentralized architectures based on blockchain and peer-to-peer networks. By distributing data storage and control across participants rather than centralized entities, decentralized systems champion transparency, user sovereignty, and resilience. Blockchain-based identities empower members to assert ownership over their digital personas and reputations without relying on a single platform's oversight. Governance tokens introduce democratic mechanisms where decisions— from policy changes to resource allocation—are collectively voted on, embedding community autonomy into code. Peer-to-peer storage circumvents censorship and reduces reliance on corporate servers, enhancing privacy and continuity. These architectures reconstruct community not as a product of corporate design but as a self-governed ecosystem responsive to its members' evolving needs.

Complementing decentralization is the developing practice of edge computing, which relocates data processing closer to users' devices. This low-latency, on-device calculation reduces dependence on distant cloud servers, resulting in faster responses and improved privacy by keeping sensitive information local. For community platforms, edge computing means real-time interaction—even in bandwidth-limited environments—and a smoother, more secure user experience. It enables localized moderation or AI personalization that respects individual autonomy, reinforcing trust without sacrificing convenience.

With these technological foundations laid, an equally important dimension emerges: predictive community management. Leveraging analytics and machine learning, platforms can now forecast patterns of engagement, churn, or conflict before they fully manifest. By identifying early warning signs of dwindling interest or brewing disputes, moderators and automated systems can intervene proactively, tailoring interventions to specific community dynamics. These foresights turn management from reactive firefighting into strategic stewardship, nurturing sustainable growth and cohesion. The challenge lies in balancing data-driven insights with ethical considerations, ensuring that prediction serves empowerment rather than manipulation.

The potential of smarter content discovery is also amplified by developments in the Semantic Web and metadata standards. By encoding relationships between concepts, people, and interests through linked data and ontologies, platforms become capable of understanding not just keywords but the underlying meaning of content and interactions. This semantic richness enhances recommendation engines and search tools, enabling users to navigate vast information landscapes intuitively and find kindred spirits or relevant knowledge effortlessly. It also cultivates serendipitous encounters—the lifeblood of vibrant communities—by surfacing unexpected connections woven through shared values or goals.

Venturing into the speculative yet increasingly tangible, the concept of digital twin communities offers an intriguing vision. Here, virtual counterparts mirror real-world organizations, neighborhoods, or event spaces, creating dynamic replicas that reflect ongoing activity through real-time data integration. These digital twins serve as experimental arenas for testing policies, simulating social dynamics, or simply extending community interaction beyond physical constraints. For instance, a city council's digital twin could engage citizens in planning discussions via virtual town halls, fostering transparency and participation on unprecedented scales. This extension blurs the boundary between online and offline, suggesting a future where communities inhabit dual realities, each enriching the other.

However, this brave new world of technological possibilities is shadowed by ethical and regulatory challenges. The power of AI to moderate and generate content raises urgent questions about bias and fairness—how to ensure systems do not amplify existing prejudices or silence marginalized voices? Decentralized governance mechanisms confront dilemmas around accountability and conflict resolution when control is diffused. Privacy concerns mount as interconnected devices and edge computing collect ever more intimate data streams. Regulatory frameworks struggle to keep pace with rapid innovation, risking either stifling experimentation or allowing unchecked harms. Navigating these tensions requires transparent design, inclusive processes, and a commitment to values that prioritize human dignity alongside efficiency.

Against this complex backdrop, a pragmatic roadmap for adoption emerges as communities experiment with integrating new technologies. Pilot programs allow careful testing of features in controlled environments, gathering user feedback and measuring impacts on engagement and trust. Scaling successful initiatives involves transparent communication and education to ease transitions and foster buy-in. Throughout, ongoing evaluation is critical, deploying both qualitative insights and quantitative metrics to balance innovation with sustainability. Ultimately, the goal is not technological novelty for its own sake but a thoughtfully crafted ecosystem where human connection thrives, supported by tools that amplify rather than diminish agency.

As these emerging technologies converge, they do more than supplement old community forms—they reinvent the very possibilities of social life. From AI-enhanced personalization to immersive realities, decentralized governance to predictive insights, the horizon is rich with potential to forge communities that are more dynamic, inclusive, and resilient. This future invites us to rethink not just how we connect, but who we become together in a digitally intertwined world.

Chapter 6

The Impact of Virtual Communities on Society

This chapter explores how virtual communities reshape the world around us: driving new modes of learning and collaboration, redefining work and professional networks, catalyzing social movements, fostering intercultural exchange, and influencing individual wellbeing. We conclude by confronting the darker side of online life—misinformation, manipulation, and groupthink—that challenges community resilience and public trust.

6.1 Learning, Knowledge Sharing, and Open Source

At the heart of the digital age lies a powerful transformation in how we learn and collaborate: the emergence of learning communities. These are groups formed not simply by physical proximity or institutional affiliation, but by a shared pursuit of knowledge, skills, or creative endeavor, often distributed across vast online networks. What distinguishes learning communities is their emphasis on active participation, mutual support, and collective growth. Far from passive recipients of information, members engage in dialogue, ask questions, share resources, and co-construct understanding. The social fabric of these communities weaves learning into a dynamic, ongoing process that transcends traditional classroom boundaries.

Within this ecosystem, contrasting modes of learning coexist. On one end, structured Massive Open Online Courses (MOOCs) offer formal, curriculum-based instruction to thousands of learners simultaneously. Their appeal lies in accessibility and a well-defined pathway through content, complete with quizzes and certificates. Yet, MOOCs can sometimes feel impersonal, resembling lectures snapped from university halls into the digital void. In contrast, informal environments— discussion forums, chat groups, coding communities— fuel peer-to-peer knowledge exchange. Here, learning is less about completing a syllabus and more about problem-solving in real time, trading tips, or exploring niche interests. This informal, emergent learning thrives on reciprocity: learners become teachers, experts evolve through dialogue, and knowledge flows in multiple directions.

Many such communities revolve around the idea of a *knowledge commons*: shared digital repositories and open-access models where resources are collectively stewarded rather than hoarded. These commons embody principles of openness—anyone can add, edit, or use the materials—with governance often maintained through transparent rules and peer oversight. For example, open research archives allow scientists worldwide to share data and publications without paywalls, accelerating discovery. Similarly, educational resources under Creative Commons licenses empower teachers and students alike to adapt and remix materials to suit diverse contexts. In this way, the knowledge commons serves as both a wellspring and a workshop, blending the generosity of sharing with the rigor of collective curation.

Open source software epitomizes these ideals in the realm of technology. The open source model rests on three pillars: transparency, meritocracy, and collaborative development. Source code is freely available for anyone to inspect, modify, and distribute, fostering trust and innovation. Contributions are judged by their quality and usefulness rather than formal credentials, allowing skilled individuals from disparate backgrounds to influence complex projects. Development platforms like GitHub enable hundreds or even thousands of contributors to coalesce around a project, managing code through version control, issue tracking, and peer review. This decentralized, iterative process often produces software that rivals or surpasses proprietary counterparts in stability and functionality—all powered by a community rather than a corporation.

Beyond code, collaboration flourishes in wiki platforms that democratize knowledge creation through joint editing. Wikis allow users to build articles, documentation, or manuals collaboratively, each participant contributing fragments that others refine over time. Such platforms balance openness with governance: editing rights might be open to all, but policies and norms guide content quality and dispute resolution. Governance structures range from volunteer editors enforcing guidelines to elected committees overseeing disputes. This flexible yet accountable approach enables wikis to scale and maintain coherence despite the chaos of countless simultaneous contributors.

Learning communities online also recreate a form of apprenticeship, digitally mediated mentorship

155

that guides novices through modeling and practice. Cognitive apprenticeship online involves experienced members demonstrating expert reasoning or skills via tutorials, webinars, screen shares, or feedback on contributions. Unlike traditional classrooms, this mentorship is often informal and distributed: learners may interact with multiple mentors across time zones and platforms, receiving tailored guidance precisely when challenges arise. This scaffolding nurtures confidence and competence, fostering not just rote learning but critical thinking and creativity.

A critical underpinning of collaborative learning and development is rigorous documentation. Shared documentation practices ensure that knowledge, procedures, and rationale are recorded, reviewed, and updated systematically. Good documentation is more than a static manual; it is a living artifact reflecting ongoing changes, discussions, and insights. Standards vary by community but often include clear writing, examples, version histories, and accessible formats. High-quality documentation reduces barriers for newcomers, accelerates problem-solving, and preserves institutional memory—an indispensable asset in global, volunteer-driven endeavors.

The motivation driving contributors to participate in these communities is multifaceted and subtle. Beyond altruism, various incentive mechanisms play a role:

- Reputation systems that highlight expertise and re-liability;

- Digital badges that recognize milestones;

- Social recognition through thank-you messages, leaderboards, or roles of responsibility.

These incentives cultivate a sense of worth and belonging, encouraging sustained engagement. Unlike traditional employment, where remuneration is monetary and formal, open collaboration taps into intrinsic motivations—curiosity, mastery, social connection—reinforced by visible, community-rooted feedback.

Measuring success in such decentralized contexts demands nuanced metrics. Simple contribution counts (number of commits, edits, posts) offer a quantitative snapshot but risk incentivizing quantity over quality. More sophisticated measures examine retention rates of active users, impact of contributions as assessed by peers, or the role of a contributor in mentoring newcomers. Some communities track how often their shared resources are used or referenced beyond their own borders, offering a proxy for influence. Consolidating these diverse metrics helps communities understand what drives vitality and how they might evolve.

Maintaining quality within open, often massively scaled knowledge communities presents ongoing challenges. Peer review, moderation, and revision processes form the arsenal against misinformation, bias, and deterioration of content. These processes rely on a distributed network of volunteers who act as gatekeepers, balancing openness with accuracy. Conflicts between contributors require thoughtful mediation, often guided by community-established rules that emphasize respect and evidence. While perfection remains elusive, iterative corrections and transparent discussion channels help sustain trustworthiness over time.

As communities grow, managing their size, diversity, and governance becomes paramount. Scaling

knowledge communities involves structuring roles—
moderators, mentors, administrators—to distribute
labor and authority. Clear policies and transparent
decision-making mechanisms ensure inclusiveness
while preventing factionalism or burnout. Technology
assists with automated tools for spam detection, content
tagging, and analytics to monitor health indicators.
Importantly, cultural norms evolve, adapting to the
challenges of scale without sacrificing the participatory
spirit that defines these groups.

Wikipedia stands as a landmark case study of such
collaborative knowledge creation. Founded in 2001
as a free encyclopedia anyone could edit, its model
blends openness with intricate community governance.
Volunteers uphold policies including neutrality,
verifiability, and no original research while resolving
disputes through discussion and consensus. Its layered
system of editors, administrators, and arbitrators
manages content quality and user conduct. Wikipedia's
growth to millions of articles in hundreds of languages
testifies to the power of collective intelligence forged
through peer collaboration, transparent processes,
and shared commitment—a beacon for learning
communities worldwide.

Together, these threads—learning communities, the
knowledge commons, open-source principles, wiki
collaboration, digital apprenticeship, documentation
norms, contributor incentives, quality control, and
scalable governance—compose the vibrant ecosystem
transforming how knowledge is created, shared,
and sustained. This ecosystem challenges long-held
assumptions about expertise and authority, inviting
diverse voices to co-author the future of learning,
research, and innovation.

6.2 Work, Remote Collaboration, and Professional Networks

The past decade has witnessed a profound transformation in how work is organized and experienced. The traditional office, with its cubicles and watercoolers, is giving way to an increasingly virtual landscape where teams span continents and colleagues may have never shared the same room. This shift to distributed workforces has accelerated dramatically, driven not only by technological advances but also by cultural changes and global circumstances. Virtual communities have emerged as pivotal arenas for professional activity, reshaping relationships, teamwork, and career trajectories in ways that continue to unfold.

At its core, the rise of remote work stems from a confluence of factors: faster internet, cloud computing, and the proliferation of collaborative tools, combined with a growing appetite for flexibility and access to talent beyond geographic limits. What was once a niche arrangement for freelancers and global corporations alike is now mainstream, challenging workplace conventions while opening fresh possibilities for inclusivity and innovation. No longer confined to a single location, teams operate virtually—whether fully remote, hybrid, or distributed across multiple time zones—redefining the meaning of presence and engagement.

Central to these new modes of working is the concept of the virtual office, which exists in two complementary models: synchronous and asynchronous. Synchronous virtual workrooms mimic the immediacy of physical offices, leveraging video calls, instant messaging, and shared whiteboards to bring participants together in real time. This approach supports dynamic brainstorming, quick feedback loops, and the social spontaneity

159

typically lost outside face-to-face environments. However, it also demands coordination of schedules and can generate fatigue from constant digital interaction. On the other hand, asynchronous virtual workspaces prioritize flexibility, allowing collaborators to contribute on their own rhythms through emails, recorded updates, cloud documents, and project management boards. This model empowers global teams to avoid the tyranny of time zones and deepens focus by reducing the pressure of instantaneous response, though it requires clear expectations and robust documentation to prevent miscommunication.

The architecture of these virtual offices relies heavily on collaboration platforms that have become indispensable in modern professional life. Slack, Microsoft Teams, and similar tools create digital hubs where conversations, files, and workflows converge, enabling seamless exchange across departments and roles. In software development, platforms like GitHub provide not just code repositories but forums for review and iteration, fostering transparent, collective ownership over complex projects. These environments often blend synchronous chats with asynchronous threads, embedding notifications, tagging, and search functions to maintain coherence amid the flood of data. Rather than replacing human connection, such tools scaffold interactions, ensuring that geography rarely limits the speed or quality of teamwork.

Beyond coordination, the fabric of professional relationships is increasingly woven through dedicated networking sites, of which LinkedIn is the most prominent example. These platforms transcend mere contact lists, serving as dynamic ecosystems for skill validation, reputation building, and opportunity discovery. Profiles that highlight certifications, endorsements, project histories, and thought leadership act as digital CVs accessible across industries and borders. Recruiters and employers scan these networks not only for credentials but also for cultural fit and personal branding, insights deepened by shared groups and interactions. Furthermore, specialized communities—ranging from design forums to data science cohorts—offer spaces for niche expertise to flourish, fostering mentorship, collaboration, and informal learning that fuel career growth outside traditional hierarchies.

Integral to success in these environments is the cultivation of a digital professional identity. Unlike the static résumé of the past, online personas blend portfolios, social media presence, and contributions to community knowledge bases. Thoughtful curation of this identity involves showcasing skills, values, and achievements with authenticity, balancing personal voice and professionalism. Reputation mechanisms embedded in platforms—such as endorsements, badges, and peer reviews—bring a new dimension to credibility, often influencing hiring decisions and contract opportunities. In dispersed teams, where trust is built through digital artifacts rather than chance encounters, the ability to manage visibility and narrative becomes a critical career asset.

Remote collaboration extends not only to work execution but also to onboarding and training, an area once heavily dependent on in-person immersion. Remote induction now leans on comprehensive documentation, recorded orientations, and structured mentorship programs conducted online. New hires access rich knowledge repositories, interactive tutorials, and scheduled check-ins that replace coffee chats and shadowing. Peer support takes on heightened importance; virtual

buddies or team mentors provide social scaffolding and
culture transmission through continuous feedback and
informal conversations. These practices mitigate the
risks of isolation and ambiguity, crucial for integrating
talent effectively when physical proximity is absent.

Effective distributed teams also innovate in decision-
making processes to accommodate their asynchronous
nature. Instead of relying solely on hierarchical top-
down mandates, many adopt consensus-building
approaches that leverage collective input across time
zones. Delegated authority empowers individuals or
small groups to act within defined domains, accelerating
responsiveness without sacrificing oversight. Approval
workflows often unfold asynchronously, using shared
documents with comment chains or specialized tools
that record rationale and track changes transparently.
This diffusion of decision power challenges traditional
organizational models, promoting agility and inclusivity
but demanding discipline in communication and
accountability to avoid confusion or gridlock.

Trust and accountability become linchpins in virtual
work arrangements, where spontaneous supervision
is impossible. Teams employ dashboards to visualize
progress, making key metrics visible to all members
and stakeholders. Regular status updates—whether
video snippets, chat summaries, or task boards—create
a rhythm of check-ins that build confidence in shared
goals and individual contributions. Retrospectives
at project milestones serve not only for performance
assessment but also for collective reflection, surfacing
insights into both technical hurdles and interpersonal
dynamics. When transparency is embedded into
the workflow, trust flourishes even in the absence of
physical presence, sustaining motivation and cohesion.

Measuring productivity in such dispersed and diverse

contexts is another evolving challenge. Traditional
time-based metrics give way to assessments focused
on deliverables, cycle times, and peer evaluations. The
emphasis shifts from hours logged to outcomes
realized, encouraging autonomy and creativity.
Engagement levels, captured through participation
in meetings, discussions, and collaborative editing,
provide additional signals of team health. While
data-driven approaches can illuminate bottlenecks
and achievements, they must be complemented by
qualitative understanding of context to avoid reductive
judgments that overlook the complexity of knowledge
work.

The recruitment landscape has also expanded beyond
resumes and interviews, harnessing online community
engagement to identify talent. Contributions to
open-source projects, participation in hackathons,
and active involvement in technical forums serve
as living portfolios demonstrating skill, problem-
solving ability, and cultural fit. This shift facilitates
discovery of candidates outside conventional pipelines,
democratizing access to opportunities and enabling
organizations to tap into rich, diverse talent pools
worldwide. Moreover, community-driven recruitment
fosters ongoing relationships where individuals grow
into roles, supported by networks that validate and
amplify their expertise.

Yet the always-on nature of virtual collaboration blurs
boundaries between work and personal life, posing
risks to wellbeing. Strategies for managing this overlap
include setting explicit temporal limits, cultivating
rituals that mark transitions, and prioritizing offline
recovery. Organizations that acknowledge these
dynamics encourage asynchronous communication,
respect individual rhythms, and promote mental health

resources. Cultivating a culture where "disconnecting" is normalized helps prevent burnout and preserves long-term productivity, recognizing that human sustainability underpins technological progress.

Despite its promise, remote collaboration presents notable challenges. Miscommunications arise easily without nonverbal cues, making clarity and patience essential virtues. Time-zone differences complicate scheduling, sometimes forcing inconvenient hours or fragmenting team cohesion. Social isolation can erode engagement and creativity, prompting the need for intentional community-building and informal interactions, whether through virtual coffee breaks or team games. Addressing these issues requires continual adaptation, empathy, and investment in tools and practices designed to bridge the gaps left by physical absence.

In sum, virtual communities have become the new terrain upon which professional relationships, distributed teams, and careers are constructed and navigated. They dissolve geographical constraints, multiplying both possibilities and complexities in equal measure. Navigating this evolving ecosystem demands not only technical proficiency but also new literacies of communication, collaboration, and self-presentation. As these digital workspaces mature, they invite us to rethink fundamental assumptions about presence, identity, and achievement, reshaping the very fabric of professional life in the twenty-first century.

6.3 Social Movements and Digital Activism

The face of activism has undergone a profound transformation with the rise of digital technologies, ushering in a new era often termed *digital activism*. Unlike traditional protest modalities—such as marches, sit-ins, or leafleting—digital activism leverages the global connectivity of the internet to mobilize, communicate, and advocate for change. This form of activism blurs geographical boundaries and temporal constraints, allowing individuals to participate in social and political causes from anywhere and at any time. While conventional activism typically depends upon physical presence and direct confrontation, digital activism often uses online tools to amplify voices, craft narratives, and coordinate collective actions. This shift does not render traditional activism obsolete; rather, it complements and sometimes reinvents it, expanding the repertoire of resistance and solidarity.

At the core of digital activism lies the creation of networked public spheres enabled by social media platforms, discussion forums, and dedicated websites. These digital arenas function as modern agoras where ideas are debated and identities forged. Unlike traditional mass media, which tend to be top-down and gatekept, online spaces are interactive and decentralized, allowing ordinary users to generate and circulate content widely and rapidly. Twitter threads, Facebook groups, Reddit conversations, and TikTok videos become venues where marginalized voices may find resonance and where grassroots narratives rival official accounts. This democratization of discourse reshapes power dynamics, enabling movements to bypass institutional barriers and reach diverse audiences. However, it also raises challenges of misinformation, echo chambers, and platform biases, making the digital public sphere both a site of hope and contest.

One of the pivotal ways online communities foster social movements is through the construction of collective

165

identity and the strategic framing of issues. Digital
campaigns craft narratives that resonate emotionally
and intellectually, helping participants see themselves
as part of a larger "we." This process—known as
identity framing—is crucial for building solidarity. For
example, hashtags, slogans, and shared stories serve
as rallying points that transform disparate individuals
into cohesive activist networks. Emphasizing common
grievances, aspirations, and values, digital framing
can galvanize supporters around causes ranging from
racial justice to climate action. This sense of belonging
is especially potent in dispersed movements where
physical gatherings are limited; the virtual sense
of community nurtures commitment and sustained
participation.

Hashtag activism exemplifies the power of digital
mobilization and the viral nature of online solidarity.
Campaigns like #MeToo and #BlackLivesMatter
illustrate how succinct, catchy tags can crystallize
complex social issues into accessible rallying cries.
#MeToo, which emerged as a platform for survivors
of sexual violence to share their experiences, rapidly
expanded into a global movement exposing systemic
abuses and catalyzing policy debates. Similarly,
#BlackLivesMatter, born from outrage against police
violence, became a symbol of racial justice struggles
worldwide. These hashtags do more than trend;
they create expansive online communities that share
testimonies, organize protests, and drive political
dialogues. Their success lies in amplifying marginalized
voices and pressuring institutions while enabling
millions to engage with the cause through simple acts
of sharing or posting.

Beyond awareness-raising, online activism offers
concrete tools for fast and effective mobilization through

petitions and crowdfunding platforms. Digital petitions harness the collective power of signatures to pressure policymakers or corporations, often achieving visibility and milestones unattainable through traditional paper-based methods. Sites like Change.org facilitate this process globally, enabling local campaigns to tap into international solidarity. Meanwhile, crowdfunding platforms such as GoFundMe or Kickstarter allow movements to gather financial resources quickly, supporting legal defenses, event logistics, or grassroots journalism. These tools lower barriers to participation and resource acquisition, translating virtual support into actionable momentum.

The architecture of online activism also enhances coordination praxis. Digital tools now enable event planning, virtual town halls, and volunteer management at scales previously unimaginable. Platforms like Slack, Telegram, or Discord provide encrypted and organized spaces where activists can strategize, allocate roles, and disseminate real-time information during protests or campaigns. More so, live streaming and interactive webinars create participatory forums that nurture transparency and collective decision-making. Such coordination technologies complement on-the-ground efforts by synchronizing dispersed contributors, maintaining engagement, and adapting quickly to evolving political contexts.

Tactics deployed by digital activists have evolved considerably, reflecting both creativity and technological innovation. Memes—an intersection of humor, culture, and political commentary—have become ubiquitous tools to critique power or spread messages virally and memorably. Viral videos, often shot on smartphones, capture moments of injustice or solidarity and amplify them globally, sometimes provoking urgent public responses or legal investigations. More recently, augmented reality (AR) and virtual reality (VR) have been experimented with to stage immersive protests or simulate lived experiences of oppression, thus expanding the activist toolkit's sensory and emotional reach. This continual reinvention of tactics illustrates digital activism's dynamic nature and its capacity to adapt symbolic repertoires to new media environments.

Yet, the digital activism landscape is not without critique, particularly concerning the phenomenon termed *slacktivism*. This term captures the tension between low-effort online support—such as liking, sharing, or retweeting—and the deeper, sustained engagement required for meaningful change. While digital gestures can signify solidarity and raise awareness, they sometimes risk replacing more demanding actions like volunteering, organizing, or direct confrontation. Critics warn that slacktivism may create an illusion of participation that placates rather than empowers. However, defenders argue that online engagement often serves as a gateway, mobilizing interest that can translate into offline activism. Understanding this balance remains essential for evaluating the efficacy and ethics of digital movements.

Alongside these opportunities are significant chal-lenges posed by censorship and digital repression. Authoritarian regimes and even democratic states have developed sophisticated techniques for surveillance, content takedowns, blocking access, or spreading disinformation targeted at activist communities. Platforms themselves sometimes comply with government requests to remove political content or disrupt organizing efforts, inadvertently facilitating digital censorship. Activists face risks not only of losing platforms but also of exposure and retaliation through hacking, doxing, or legal harassment. This hostile environment requires ongoing vigilance, technical innovation (such as encryption), and international solidarity to protect digital freedoms as a precondition for effective activism.

Ethical considerations in digital activism extend beyond security to include privacy, consent, and responsible campaigning. The ease of sharing information can lead to unintended harms, such as doxing—the public exposure of private information—which may endanger individuals or communities. Campaigns must navigate the tension between transparency for legitimacy and the protection of vulnerable participants. Moreover, the use of bots or manipulative tactics to artificially inflate support raises questions about authenticity and integrity. Ethical digital activism prioritizes respectful engagement, informed consent, and strategies that empower rather than exploit participants or audiences.

The lessons learned from defining moments of digital activism are instructive for understanding its full potential and limits. The Arab Spring uprisings of the early 2010s showcased how social media could accelerate political mobilization across countries with repressive regimes, enabling rapid dissemination of information and coordination of protests. Yet, the aftermath also revealed the fragility of digital movements under state crackdowns and the difficulty of translating momentary euphoria into sustainable democratic change. Similarly, climate justice networks have effectively harnessed online tools to organize global days of action, educate the public, and demand policy responses. These cases exemplify both the promise and complexity of digital activism as a force for social transformation.

Together, these facets demonstrate how online commu-

nities act as powerful incubators of mobilization, solidarity, and collective action. By weaving together narrative
framing, viral communication, rapid resource mobilization, and real-time coordination, digital activism transcends traditional limitations and reimagines the possibilities of political engagement. Yet, it remains an evolving terrain embedded within broader social, technological, and political contests—one that demands critical attention to its dynamics, tactics, and ethical implications.

6.4 Cultural Exchange and Globaliza-
tion

The advent of virtual communities has transformed the
landscape of cultural exchange, making globalization
not just an economic or political phenomenon, but a
vividly social and interactive process. Online networks
serve as vast conduits where ideas, art, and customs
traverse borders with unprecedented speed and reach.
This digital cultural diffusion amplifies the flow of
human creativity far beyond traditional geographical
constraints, enabling an ongoing dialogue across
continents and cultures.

At its core, digital cultural diffusion involves the sharing,
remixing, and adaptation of cultural elements through
platforms ranging from social media and video-sharing
sites to forums and immersive virtual worlds. For
instance, the viral spread of dance trends, cuisine
recipes, or storytelling styles illustrates how a local
tradition can rapidly become a global phenomenon.
Such exchanges do not merely replicate cultural
artifacts—they transform them, as they are interpreted
by individuals with different backgrounds, creating
hybrid forms that enrich the global cultural fabric. Yet,
this process is not unidirectional; it fosters a pluralism

where multiple voices contribute to a living, evolving tapestry of shared human expression.

However, the promise of intercultural dialogue faces practical challenges, particularly regarding communication. Language barriers remain a persistent obstacle, but technology offers inventive solutions. Automated translation tools, while imperfect, have steadily improved, enabling real-time conversations that would have been unimaginable even a decade ago. In virtual communities, code-switching—the practice of alternating between languages or dialects within a conversation—is a common adaptation that facilitates mutual understanding. Users often blend languages or adopt pidgin forms, reflecting the fluid and dynamic nature of intercultural communication online. These linguistic negotiations reveal not only practical strategies but also a willingness to engage empathetically with different cultural perspectives.

Nevertheless, digital cultural exchange is not without its pitfalls. The risk of cultural appropriation—a process where elements of a minority culture are borrowed and commodified by dominant groups without proper recognition or respect—remains a critical concern. Such imbalances often mirror offline power relations, with dominant cultures able to extract or distort cultural symbols for entertainment or profit, sometimes causing offense or erasure. Responsible cultural exchange requires an awareness of context, consent, and mutual respect, reminding us that sharing culture is not merely about access, but about ethical engagement and recognition of the histories behind these expressions.

Virtual spaces also serve as vital lifelines for diaspora and heritage communities, offering refuge from isolation and a means to sustain cultural identity. Expatriates and migrants increasingly rely on online platforms to

171

maintain social ties, celebrate traditions, and transmit language and customs across generations. Virtual storytelling circles, digital family archives, and live-streamed religious ceremonies are just a few ways these communities nurture heritage irrespective of physical distance. Such practices demonstrate how technology not only diffuses culture but anchors it, creating digital homes that coexist with, rather than replace, physical ones.

Global fandoms provide another remarkable example of cultural globalization. Enthusiasts united by interest in media franchises, sports, or hobbies form transnational communities that co-create meaning and belonging. Whether through fan fiction, online tournaments, or synchronized watch parties, these groups engage in a participatory culture that transcends national boundaries. They often become cultural brokers, introducing and interpreting content for diverse audiences, facilitating dialogue among fans with varying backgrounds, and celebrating both shared passions and the multiplicity of cultural interpretations.

Shared virtual rituals further illustrate how technology enables global participation in events that foster collective identity. International festivals broadcast live, collaborative art projects connecting creators across continents, and synchronous commemorations demonstrate how digital platforms can summon communal spirit without physical presence. These rituals leverage the affordances of the internet to create moments of synchronous engagement, weaving together participants from disparate time zones and cultures into a shared experience that is at once local and global.

Such synchronous coordination across multiple time zones demands thoughtful strategies. Scheduling online events, whether meetings or global festivals, must navigate differences in work hours, social habits, and cultural norms regarding time. Successful virtual gatherings often depend on flexibility, including rotating event times, asynchronous participation options, and clear communication about expectations. These adaptive tactics underscore the complexity of fostering true global collaboration, requiring not only technological infrastructure but sensitivity to cultural rhythms and practices.

Digital cosmopolitanism emerges from this interconnectedness as a framework for understanding hybrid identities forged in the crucible of globalized online interactions. Participants in virtual communities frequently develop senses of belonging that cross national or ethnic lines, embracing a shared commitment to global citizenship. This hybridity challenges traditional notions of identity as fixed or singular, instead portraying it as fluid, multiple, and negotiated through interaction. The virtual world becomes a testing ground and catalyst for new forms of social cohesion—ones that celebrate cultural diversity while seeking common ground.

The operational backbone of maintaining these rich, diverse communities often lies in multilingual moderation. Effective moderation requires adapting guidelines and tools to respect linguistic and cultural differences, ensuring that communication remains respectful and inclusive. Moderators may need to confront varied norms about directness, humor, or conflict and develop culturally aware strategies to foster dialogue rather than division. Intelligent use of translation, culturally sensitive conflict resolution, and inclusive decision-making help create virtual spaces where diverse communities feel valued and heard.

Finally, the collaborative potential unlocked by global virtual communities extends well beyond social and cultural dimensions into practical realms. Open-source software projects, international scientific research consortia, and transnational volunteer networks exemplify how collaboration across borders can address shared challenges innovatively. In such projects, participants contribute specialized knowledge and perspectives grounded in their cultural contexts, enhancing creativity and problem-solving. This synergy exemplifies how cultural exchange facilitated by virtual communities not only enriches individual identities but can produce tangible, collective benefits on a global scale.

Together, these interconnected phenomena illustrate how virtual communities act as vibrant crucibles of cultural exchange in an era of globalization. They foster dialogue and creativity, bridge linguistic and geographic divides, and cultivate new forms of collective identity and cooperation. Yet they also invite us to remain mindful of power dynamics and ethical responsibilities that underpin genuine intercultural engagement. Understanding these complexities enriches our appreciation of digital culture as a dynamic, sometimes messy but always fascinating terrain where the world's cultures meet, mingle, and transform.

6.5 Mental Health: Benefits and Pitfalls

Community participation has long been recognized as a double-edged sword in shaping mental wellbeing. On the one hand, engaging with others offers a vital source of social support; on the other, it can expose individuals to harm, stress, or unhealthy patterns. By exploring how communal involvement influences psychological health, we can appreciate not only the power of connection but also the careful balance required to protect mental resilience.

One of the clearest benefits of community participation lies in the formation of peer support networks. Groups such as mental health forums, peer-led support circles, and empathy-based gatherings provide spaces where individuals share experiences, exchange coping strategies, and offer validation. These environments foster mutual understanding, breaking the isolating silence often surrounding mental health struggles. For instance, an online forum dedicated to anxiety management allows participants from diverse backgrounds to find common ground and reassurance, which can significantly reduce feelings of loneliness. Empathy circles, where attentive listening without judgment is the norm, create a rare psychological sanctuary, reinforcing the idea that one is neither unusual nor unsupported in their challenges.

Beyond support, a sense of belonging emerges as a potent contributor to wellbeing. When individuals feel included within communities—be they social clubs, faith groups, or interest-based collectives—the psychological benefits reverberate through elevated self-esteem and greater resilience to stress. Belonging acts as a social anchor; it nurtures identity by embedding personal narratives within a collective story. This is especially impactful for marginalized groups or those recovering from trauma, for whom community inclusion affirms worth and counters alienation. Resilience nurtured in such contexts is not simply the ability to endure difficulties, but the confidence to confront and grow from them, sustained by a network of shared human connection.

Interestingly, the structure of community participation can also facilitate disclosure in ways that enhance safety. Anonymity and pseudonymity, especially in digital settings, often encourage individuals to share sensitive or stigmatized experiences without fear of judgment or repercussion. This protective veil enables people to reveal vulnerabilities, seek advice, or simply vent their emotions in a secure environment. For some, the opportunity to speak openly—even under a false name—can be transformative, fostering honesty that might otherwise be suppressed in face-to-face interactions. Such anonymous exchanges become a form of collective healing, where empathy flows unhampered by fears tied to identity or reputation.

Yet, the very platforms that enable safe disclosure can harbor darker risks. Exposure to harassment, hate speech, and triggering content is a persistent threat, particularly in loosely regulated spaces. Cyberbullying— ranging from subtle exclusion to overt verbal abuse—can exacerbate existing mental health issues or precipitate new ones. Additionally, communities sometimes inadvertently circulate media that evoke traumatic memories or heighten distress, compounding individual suffering. The emotional toll from encountering hostility or harmful material highlights that community participation is not universally beneficial; it requires safeguards to function as a source of wellbeing rather than harm.

The increasing prevalence of digital connectivity introduces another protective challenge: overengagement. Addiction to social platforms or compulsive group involvement can lead to burnout, anxiety, and a persistent fear of missing out (FOMO). Paradoxically, belonging too intensively to multiple communities may fragment attention and impede restorative solitude.

Constant notifications and the pressure to respond instantly embed stress into daily life, undermining mental balance. This relentless connectivity can blur the boundary between healthy participation and exhaustion, underscoring the need for mindful moderation of one's communal interactions.

Recognizing these pitfalls, many platforms and communities are adopting design strategies specifically aimed at fostering wellbeing. Features such as time-out reminders encourage users to pause and reflect rather than remain endlessly engaged. Content filters help shield participants from triggering material or toxic language, while mental health check-ins invite individuals to self-assess and seek support when needed. These design choices represent an intentional effort to create environments that respect psychological needs, promoting sustained and positive participation rather than reactive or damaging involvement.

Community safety also hinges on effective moderation. Proactive moderators who monitor discussions, remove harmful content, and mediate conflicts play a crucial role in maintaining a supportive atmosphere. Importantly, moderation today extends beyond censorship—it includes linking participants with crisis resources and professional support when warning signs emerge. By connecting community members with helplines or counseling services, moderators act as gatekeepers not only of discussion quality but also of wellbeing pathways. Such integrative approaches transform communities from mere conversation spaces into networks of care.

Nevertheless, even with thoughtful design and moderation, conscious disengagement remains vital. Digital detox strategies—such as scheduled breaks, silent hours, or reduced screen time—help counterbalance the intensity of online participation. These practices foster awareness of how communal involvement affects mood and energy, empowering individuals to reclaim control over their interactions. Offline activities, mindfulness exercises, and physical social encounters complement digital engagement by restoring equilibrium and reinforcing diverse sources of wellbeing.

Increasingly, successful community participation is complemented by professional mental health integration. Collaborations between online groups and therapists, counselors, or helplines enhance the reliability of support offered. Professional involvement ensures that individuals facing acute difficulties encounter appropriate interventions beyond peer encouragement. For instance, some mental health platforms provide direct access to licensed therapists via chat functions or schedule referrals triggered by user disclosures. This blending of community solidarity with expert care forms a comprehensive scaffold that strengthens both prevention and recovery.

To navigate this complex landscape effectively, measuring wellbeing within communities is essential. Methods include surveys gauging participant satisfaction and stress levels, sentiment analysis exploring emotional tone in discussions, and self-report scales tracking mood changes over time. Such tools offer valuable feedback to community organizers and designers about what promotes mental health and where vulnerabilities lie. Continuous assessment helps tailor environments to evolving needs, ensuring that communities grow in ways that maximize benefits and minimize risks.

Ultimately, community participation is neither a panacea nor a peril in isolation. Its impact on mental health emerges from a dynamic interplay between individual needs, group culture, technological design, and external support structures. When nurtured with care and attention to both human connection and psychological safety, communities become fertile ground for empathy, identity, and growth. Yet the same spaces, without balance and vigilance, may amplify distress or foster unhealthy dependencies. Appreciating this spectrum equips us to engage with communities thoughtfully, turning participation into a source of strength rather than strain.

6.6 Misinformation, Manipulation, and Groupthink

In the sprawling digital agora of today's virtual spaces, the exchange of information is swift, vast, and often unchecked. Within this torrent, the line between truth and falsehood blurs, propelled by forces both organic and orchestrated. To navigate this landscape, it is essential first to understand the key distinctions: *misinformation* and *disinformation*. Misinformation refers to false or misleading information shared without the intent to deceive—often arising from error or misunderstanding. Disinformation, in contrast, is deliberately crafted and disseminated to mislead or manipulate. Recognizing this difference matters because it shapes how we react; combating unintentional errors requires education, while intentional deception demands vigilance and accountability.

Yet the challenge extends beyond the content's nature to how it spreads. Information cascades describe a phenomenon where individuals, seeing others endorse a claim, accept it themselves regardless of their own information or judgment. When false beliefs ignite such cascades—rapid, self-reinforcing chains of acceptance—they become deeply entrenched and resistant to correction. This effect is amplified in social media environments, where speed and visibility can turn a baseless rumor into collective "knowledge" within hours, sometimes minutes. The urgency and volume of shares overwhelm critical scrutiny, allowing inaccuracies to sediment into popular consensus.

Compounding these dynamics are the darker mechanisms of digital influence: automated accounts known as *bots* and human-operated *trolls*. Bots operate tirelessly, generating or amplifying content to artificially inflate popularity or give the illusion of broad agreement. Paid trolls, by contrast, manipulate discussions with targeted messages designed to sow discord, confuse, or promote specific agendas. Together, they distort the social media ecosystem by manufacturing activity and framing narratives in ways that seem authentic but are meticulously engineered. These operations exploit the very architecture of virtual spaces, exploiting human cognitive biases and social norms to shift opinion surreptitiously.

This leads naturally to the role of platform algorithms— recommendation engines that curate what users see based on engagement metrics and inferred preferences. While designed to enhance user experience, these algorithms often elevate content that provokes strong emotional reactions, such as outrage or sensationalism. As a result, false or misleading information that triggers such responses tends to receive disproportionate exposure, further accelerating its spread. This *algorithmic amplification* turns misinformation from isolated incidents into viral phenomena, effectively rewarding shock value over accuracy. It creates a feedback loop where engagement drives visibility, and visibility drives engagement, regardless of truthfulness.

Within these algorithmically shaped landscapes, users

increasingly find themselves enveloped in *filter bubbles* and *echo chambers*. Filter bubbles arise when personalization, based on past behavior and preferences, limits the diversity of information encountered. Echo chambers intensify this effect by surrounding individuals with like-minded viewpoints, reinforcing existing biases and minimizing exposure to opposing perspectives. Both phenomena contribute to social fragmentation and polarization by insulating groups from challenge and diluting the incentives for critical reflection. Instead of fostering dialogue, these insulated clusters can become echoic arenas where misconceptions flourish through mutual reinforcement.

The social processes at work inside these homogeneous groups often reflect the classic dynamics of *groupthink*. Originating from social psychology, groupthink describes a mode of collective thinking where the desire for consensus overrides critical appraisal of alternative ideas. In the context of virtual spaces, tight-knit online communities exert pressures toward conformity, encouraging self-censorship and discouraging dissenting voices. The fear of ostracization or argument fatigue leads participants to prioritize harmony over accuracy or thorough debate. This environment stifles intellectual diversity and cultivates rigid norms, making the group vulnerable to collective errors and blind spots.

In this fraught environment, discerning trustworthy information becomes paramount. *Trust signals* serve as essential markers in this pursuit—these include established reputations of sources, clear citations, and transparent methodologies. Credible journalism, scholarly references, and firsthand accounts typically exhibit such signals, which help users differentiate between well-founded claims and dubious assertions.

However, the digital inundation and the sophistication
of deceptive tactics can obscure these markers, requiring
users to maintain heightened awareness and skepticism
in assessing information.

To counter falsehoods at scale, *fact-checking communities*
have emerged as grassroots and institutional actors
committed to verification and debunking. These
groups leverage collective intelligence and crowdsourcing techniques to identify, analyze, and correct
misinformation rapidly. Their efforts often involve
collaboration across borders and disciplines, reinforcing
the idea that truth-seeking is a shared responsibility.
By exposing inaccuracies and providing context, fact-
checkers help inoculate the public against erroneous
beliefs and reduce the impact of misinformation
cascades.

Education plays a crucial role in augmenting these
efforts. *Digital literacy* initiatives focus on equipping
individuals with the skills needed to critically
evaluate online content, identify logical fallacies, and
understand the mechanics behind information flows.
Training programs and resources guide users through
recognizing subtle manipulations, cross-checking
sources, and maintaining a balanced information diet.
Such empowerment fosters resilience by transforming
passive consumers into active, discerning participants
in digital discourse.

Recognizing their duty, platforms themselves have
deployed various *countermeasures* to slow or neutralize
the spread of harmful content. These include labeling
posts with warnings, downranking sensational or
disputed material to reduce visibility, and enabling
users to report misinformation. Some platforms
also provide direct links to authoritative resources
alongside contested claims. While imperfect and often

controversial in their scope and enforcement, these tools signal an ongoing attempt to balance open expression with responsibility, a complex tension inherent to large-scale digital ecosystems.

Beyond technical fixes, *regulatory and ethical responses* offer frameworks to govern online speech and accountability. Policies range from legislation requiring transparency in political advertising to moderation mandates aimed at curbing hate speech and misinformation. Ethical design principles advocate for platforms to prioritize user well-being over engagement metrics and to embed safeguards that respect privacy and promote diverse viewpoints. These approaches underscore the societal dimension of the problem, recognizing that digital manipulation and misinformation are not merely technical issues but deeply entwined with governance, rights, and democratic values.

Finally, fostering *resilience* within communities is vital to counteract groupthink and manipulation from within. Practical strategies include encouraging diverse sourcing—actively seeking contradicting perspectives—and adopting *devil's advocacy* to challenge prevailing assumptions. Promoting open dialogue, tolerating dissent, and nurturing critical reflection create environments where false consensus is less likely to take hold. In this way, community practices become a powerful bulwark against the psychological and social dynamics that enable misinformation to thrive.

Together, these interlocking phenomena and responses reveal the complexity of confronting misinformation, manipulation, and groupthink in virtual spaces. The challenge transcends the battle against false facts, extending into the architecture of technology, the psychology of social behavior, and the norms of

collective decision-making.   Navigating this territory
demands awareness, care, and collaborative effort—not
only from platforms and policymakers but from every
individual seeking truth amid the noise.

Chapter 7

Ethics, Risks, and Governance

This chapter addresses the ethical imperatives, potential harms, and governance frameworks necessary to sustain healthy virtual communities. We begin by defining digital citizenship and individual responsibility, then examine privacy, data protection, and surveillance. Next, we explore strategies to combat abuse and exclusion, and balance freedom of expression with the need to prevent harm. We then navigate legal aspects and platform liability, and conclude with design principles for equity, inclusion, and fairness online.

7.1 Digital Citizenship and Responsibility

The internet is not merely a network of computers; it is a bustling social ecosystem where every participant assumes the role of a digital citizen. Digital citizenship encompasses more than just accessing technology—it embodies a set of rights, duties, and ethical behaviors that shape how we interact, communicate, and coexist online. Just as citizenship in a nation involves privileges balanced by obligations, digital citizenship demands that we engage responsibly in virtual communities, respecting others while safeguarding our own freedoms.

This dynamic equilibrium of individual expression and collective norms forms the foundation of responsible participation in the digital world.

At the core of digital citizenship lie fundamental rights that users expect to exercise online. Chief among these is the right to free expression—the ability to share ideas, opinions, and creativity without undue censorship. Alongside this is the right to privacy, the control over personal information and protection from unwarranted surveillance or data exploitation. However, these rights are inseparable from equally vital responsibilities. The right to speak freely carries with it the duty to respect the voices of others, avoiding harassment, misinformation, or hate speech. Similarly, privacy rights coexist with the obligation to handle others' data ethically and conscientiously. Responsible digital citizens recognize that rights are not privileges enjoyed in isolation but are intertwined with reciprocal duties that uphold the integrity and health of online spaces.

To navigate these complex interactions, various ethical frameworks offer valuable lenses through which to evaluate online conduct. A utilitarian approach asks us to consider the consequences of our actions, striving for the greatest good for the greatest number—for instance, avoiding spreading false information that could harm many. Deontological ethics, by contrast, focuses on adherence to moral rules or duties, such as honesty and respect, regardless of outcomes. Meanwhile, virtue ethics emphasizes cultivating character traits like kindness, patience, and fairness as guiding principles in digital behavior. These philosophical perspectives enrich our understanding of how to act ethically in the fluid and often ambiguous context of online culture, where decisions reverberate widely and rapidly.

One of the defining features of digital engagement is the

creation of a *digital footprint*—the trail of data left by our activities online. Every comment, photo, and click contributes to an accumulating record that can persist indefinitely. This permanence means that actions once taken casually or anonymously can surface later, influencing personal reputation, professional opportunities, and social trust. Awareness of this enduring footprint serves as a powerful deterrent against reckless behavior and reminds users that accountability extends beyond the moment of posting. The internet never truly forgets, making prudence and foresight essential virtues in maintaining a respectable digital presence.

Alongside ethical awareness, responsible digital citizenship requires *digital competence*—the skills and knowledge to navigate online environments thoughtfully. This includes critical evaluation of information sources to discern fact from misinformation, technical understanding to manage privacy settings, and communication skills to engage respectfully in discussions. Competent users contribute positively by sharing accurate information, supporting constructive dialogues, and participating in communities with an informed perspective. Digital literacy thus empowers individuals not only to protect themselves but also to enrich collective experiences and foster trustworthy networks of interaction.

Communities within the digital realm often formalize their expectations through *community guidelines*, explicit codes of conduct that articulate acceptable behaviors and outline consequences for violations. These guidelines function as the rulebook by which members agree to abide, forming the institutional backbone of safe and welcoming spaces. However, the social fabric extends beyond written rules: there exists an implicit *social contract* grounded in mutual respect, cooperation, and shared responsibility. This unwritten agreement binds users together in a cooperative spirit, encouraging them to uphold norms and intervene when those norms are threatened. The combination of codified directives and tacit understandings sustains order and nurtures a sense of belonging.

Taking this one step further, *community stewardship* involves active efforts by members to maintain and enhance the digital environment. Such stewardship may manifest as volunteering to moderate discussions, reporting harmful content, or creating educational resources that elevate community standards. These contributions embody a collective investment in the health and longevity of online spaces. Stewardship reminds us that digital citizenship is not passive consumption but an engaged, ongoing commitment to cultivating positive environments where everyone can participate safely and meaningfully.

Engaging respectfully in digital discourse is both an art and a duty. Best practices for *respectful engagement* include listening attentively, responding with empathy, and remaining open to diverse perspectives. Online interactions often transcend geographic and cultural boundaries, requiring sensitivity to differing norms and experiences. Constructive dialogue thrives in atmospheres free of hostility and personal attacks, where critique focuses on ideas rather than individuals. By fostering patience and understanding, digital citizens can transform conflict into opportunity for learning and bridge divides that might otherwise harden into digital echo chambers.

Transparency and accountability form another bedrock of ethical digital citizenship. *Transparency* entails openness in decision-making processes within digital communities, from how moderation actions are carried out to how data is collected and used. When leaders and platforms communicate clearly, it builds trust and reduces confusion or suspicion. Similarly, *accountability* requires individuals to take responsibility for their contributions and interactions, acknowledging mistakes and accepting consequences. Personal disclosures—such as clarifying affiliations or correcting misstatements—enhance credibility. Together, transparency and accountability work to create a culture where honesty is valued and wrongdoing is addressed constructively.

Yet, the landscape of digital citizenship is not without ethical dilemmas that challenge simple resolutions. Anonymity, for example, can protect vulnerable voices but also shield harmful actors from accountability. Balancing privacy with safety often demands difficult trade-offs: how much surveillance is justified to prevent harm without infringing on freedoms? These tensions reveal underlying complexities where principles may conflict, requiring nuanced judgment guided by context and reflection. Navigating such quandaries calls for a flexible ethical compass, one that weighs competing values thoughtfully rather than resorting to absolutism.

Ultimately, digital citizenship and responsibility represent the evolving pact through which individuals and communities shape the character of the online world. By embracing rights with corresponding duties, grounding behavior in ethical reasoning, remaining mindful of the lasting consequences of our virtual actions, cultivating necessary competencies, and actively stewarding our digital environments, we contribute to a vibrant, respectful, and trustworthy digital society. In this shared space, every participant holds a piece of the collective puzzle—each choice echoes beyond the screen, shaping the future of how humanity connects and coexists in the digital age.

7.2 Privacy, Data, and Surveillance

In the digital age, *privacy* has become a multifaceted concept that demands careful unraveling. At its core, privacy in digital contexts means the right of individuals to control how their personal data is collected, used, and shared. It differs subtly but importantly from *confidentiality*, which refers to the protection of information from unauthorized access, and *anonymity*, where an individual's identity is intentionally obscured. Whereas confidentiality guards data from prying eyes, and anonymity removes identity tags, privacy focuses on the individual's autonomy and choice regarding information about themselves. This distinction sets the stage for understanding the complex ways our digital footprints are monitored and managed.

Personal data itself is a rich tapestry that extends beyond mere names or email addresses. We can categorize it broadly into four types:

- *Identifying data*: such as full name, date of birth, and social security number.

- *Behavioral data*: records of how one uses websites, apps, or services.

- *Metadata*: data about data, like timestamps, IP addresses, or geolocation linked to digital activity.

- *Sensitive information*: which includes health records, ethnicity, religious beliefs, or political opinions.

The collection of these sorts of data, especially when aggregated, creates detailed profiles of individuals, laying fertile ground for both personalized services and intrusive surveillance.

The journey of user data through the digital ecosystem resembles a lifecycle with several stages. It begins with *collection*, where data is gathered by websites, apps, or devices, often without users fully realizing what is being captured. From there, data moves into *storage*, housed on servers ranging from local company databases to sprawling cloud infrastructures, each with varying security standards. The *processing* stage transforms raw data into meaningful insights through algorithms, machine learning, or simple aggregation. Subsequently, data may be *shared*—legitimately with partners or, less so, with advertisers or third parties, expanding its reach. Ideally, the cycle concludes with *deletion* or anonymization, although many organizations struggle to fully erase data, leading to lingering privacy risks. Each phase introduces unique challenges for protecting user privacy, emphasizing that control over personal information is not a single act but an ongoing process.

Central to the dynamic of privacy is the notion of *consent*—how users agree to data collection and usage. Consent models vary widely, shaping the power balance between users and data collectors.

- *Explicit consent* requires a clear, informed expression from users before data gathering begins, typified by clicking "I agree" to detailed privacy terms.

- *Implicit consent* assumes agreement through continued use or passive acceptance, a model often criticized for its opacity and lack of true user understanding.

- *Informed consent* strives to present information clearly so users grasp what they authorize.

191

- *Granular consent* allows selective permission for specific data uses rather than an all-or-nothing choice.

The effectiveness of these models hinges on transparency and the practical ability for users to exercise meaningful control—something that remains a work in progress across much of the digital landscape.

Driving much of the concern around digital privacy are the *surveillance mechanisms* embedded in everyday technology. These include tracking technologies such as cookies, web beacons, and browser fingerprinting, which silently monitor users' movements across sites and apps to build detailed behavioral profiles. Corporations deploy *profiling* and *analytics* not only to tailor advertising but to influence behavior, raise engagement, and optimize services. Beyond the commercial sphere, governments engage in varying degrees of surveillance for national security, law enforcement, or social control, often justified as necessary safeguards but frequently at odds with individual rights. The intersection of these surveillance entities creates a dense web that can be difficult to navigate or resist, underscoring the importance of safeguards protecting privacy.

Given the risks of excessive data collection and prolonged storage, the principle of *data minimization* emerges as a cornerstone of privacy protection. This principle advocates that organizations should collect only the data strictly necessary for a specified purpose and retain it no longer than needed. By reducing the volume of data gathered, data minimization limits potential exposure in case of breaches and lessens the chance that information will be misused. Its elegance lies in restraint rather than complexity—a reminder that sometimes, less is truly more when it comes to preserving privacy.

To shield data throughout its lifecycle, robust *encryption and security* measures are essential. Transport Layer Security (TLS) encrypts communications over the internet, ensuring that data transmitted between users and servers cannot be easily intercepted or altered. Meanwhile, *end-to-end encryption* safeguards messages so that only the communicating parties can read their contents, a critical feature for secure messaging apps. Data *at rest*—information stored on disks or in databases—is also protected by encryption, making unauthorized access much more difficult even if storage devices are compromised. Despite these technical barriers, the effectiveness of encryption depends on rigorous implementation and user awareness, as human error and sophisticated attackers continuously challenge these defenses.

Privacy legislation has gained steam in recent years as digital privacy concerns mount, with notable examples including the *General Data Protection Regulation* (GDPR) enacted by the European Union, and the *California Consumer Privacy Act* (CCPA) in the United States. GDPR introduced sweeping rights for individuals: the right to access their data, rectify inaccuracies, erase information under certain contexts (the "right to be forgotten"), and object to profiling. It also requires organizations to justify data collection under strict lawful bases and mandates breach notifications. The CCPA, while more limited in scope, empowers Californian consumers to know what personal data is collected, request deletion, and limit its sale. Both laws have influenced privacy policy globally, inspiring new regulations and encouraging companies worldwide to adopt stronger privacy practices, thus reshaping the legal framework around digital privacy.

Privacy considerations are increasingly recognized as essential from the outset in product development and service design, formalized in the approach known as *Privacy by Design*. This philosophy embeds privacy protections into technology and business practices from conception, not as an afterthought. It emphasizes anticipatory measures such as default privacy settings favoring user control, data minimization, secure architecture, and periodic impact assessments. Privacy by Design represents a cultural shift—a proactive stance rather than reactive compliance—and promises a more respectful relationship between technology and user rights.

Complementing legal and technical frameworks are tools that enhance *user controls and transparency*, empowering individuals to manage their privacy actively. Many platforms now offer dashboards where users can review collected data, adjust privacy settings, and revoke permissions. Consent panels have grown more sophisticated, aiming to clarify what data is requested and for what purpose. Transparency reports, published by companies and governments alike, disclose how data requests and surveillance operate, fostering accountability. While these measures are steps toward rebalancing asymmetries of information and power, their real-world effectiveness hinges on design clarity and users' willingness to engage with often complex privacy options.

In sum, the interplay of data collection, consent, surveillance, and protection measures forms the battleground upon which digital privacy is won or lost. Understanding the nuances of this ecosystem—how data flows, who controls it, and what rights users possess—is vital in navigating a world where digital footprints are both currency and vulnerability. Ultimately, sustaining privacy requires vigilance,

ongoing innovation, and a commitment to respect
individual autonomy amid the ever-expanding digital
frontier.

7.3 Combating Abuse and Exclusion

Navigating digital and physical spaces with ease and
safety hinges on our ability to recognize, confront, and
dismantle various forms of abuse and exclusion. These
phenomena, often intertwined and insidious, manifest
in behaviors such as harassment, hate speech, bullying,
doxxing, and targeted attacks, each carrying distinct
yet overlapping traits that erode trust and civility.
Harassment involves persistent unwelcome behavior
aimed to intimidate or demean an individual; hate
speech targets groups based on race, religion, gender, or
other identities, fomenting division and fear; bullying
covers repeated aggressive actions that can be verbal,
physical, or psychological; doxxing—the exposure of
private information without consent—inflicts significant
harm through invasion of privacy; and targeted attacks
combine these tactics, often with organized intent, to
isolate or silence individuals or communities.

Yet abuse does not exist in a vacuum. It thrives
on exclusionary dynamics that subtly or overtly
gatekeep participation. Gatekeeping operates whenever
communities or institutions control access by arbitrarily
setting norms or qualifications, often reinforcing existing
hierarchies. Implicit bias—our unconscious attitudes
or stereotypes—further perpetuates marginalization
by influencing decisions from hiring to community
interactions. Language barriers, too, erect invisible
walls, excluding those who lack proficiency or access
to dominant communication modes. Together, these
factors create layered obstacles that systematically

disadvantage certain groups, compounding the harms of direct abuse.

Understanding exclusion necessitates an appreciation of intersectionality, a concept that illuminates how overlapping social identities—such as race, gender, class, disability, and sexuality—shape an individual's experience of discrimination and privilege. For example, a Black woman might face biases distinct from those encountered by white women or Black men, reflecting the intertwined nature of race and gender oppression. This nuanced view moves beyond single-axis frameworks, acknowledging that combating abuse and exclusion requires sensitivity to these intersecting identities to avoid solutions that inadvertently perpetuate disparities.

Detection plays a crucial role in fighting abuse, and it is an evolving blend of human judgment and technological innovation. Automated filters scan text or images for offensive content using keyword lists or pattern recognition, though these can struggle with context or novel slurs. Machine-learning classifiers, trained on vast datasets, improve detection by recognizing subtle nuances and evolving language, yet they risk false positives and algorithmic biases. Hence, human moderators remain essential, bringing empathy and contextual understanding to review flagged content, assess intent, and make balanced decisions. This hybrid approach marries speed and scale with discernment, vital for maintaining healthy spaces.

Once abuse is detected, robust reporting mechanisms empower users and foster transparency. User flagging systems enable community members to highlight problematic behavior, which can then follow escalation procedures ranging from warning notifications to account suspension or legal referral. Transparency about outcomes matters—not only to reassure complainants but also to demonstrate fairness and accountability to the wider community. Effective reporting systems must balance confidentiality, responsiveness, and clarity to build trust and encourage participation in maintaining safe environments.

Moderation strategies vary widely but share a common goal: curbing harm while preserving freedom of expression. Proactive moderation involves preemptively curating content through community guidelines and real-time monitoring, often combined with automated tools. Community-driven enforcement leverages peer accountability, where users help define norms and report violations, creating a sense of shared responsibility. Reactive takedowns occur post facto, responding swiftly to reported abuses but risking delayed intervention. Each approach bears trade-offs: proactive systems may restrict creativity but prevent escalation; community involvement nurtures engagement but can be uneven; reactive models may allow harm to persist too long. Effective moderation often blends these methods tailored to context and scale.

Creating safe spaces—moderated sanctuaries designed for vulnerable or specific groups—further counters exclusion. These environments foster trust and open dialogue by enforcing stricter rules against harassment and hate speech and offering curated support. For example, forums for survivors of trauma or minority communities provide refuge from hostile mainstream environments, allowing authentic interaction without fear. Safe spaces underscore the principle that inclusivity sometimes requires tailored boundaries rather than absolute openness.

Complementing structural measures, community

support structures are a vital layer of resilience. Peer mentoring programs connect experienced members with newcomers, providing guidance and emotional support to navigate challenges. Crisis intervention networks offer rapid help during acute abuse incidents, often linking users to professional resources. Restorative justice models emphasize repairing harm by facilitating dialogue among offenders and victims, encouraging accountability and healing over mere punishment. These approaches deepen trust, nurture empathy, and build collective capacity to withstand and recover from abuse.

Rehabilitation practices aim to reintegrate offenders through education and accountability rather than solely through exclusion. Programs that address underlying biases and harmful behaviors—whether via workshops, counseling, or monitored reintegration—seek to transform rather than merely punish. Such approaches recognize that sustainable inclusivity emerges when communities repair fractures and empower members to contribute positively, diminishing recidivism and fostering growth.

A foundational principle underlying all these efforts is accessibility and inclusion. Universal design—creating systems and environments usable by all people without adaptation—reduces barriers from the outset. This includes not only physical accessibility but also clear, multilingual communication, adaptive technologies for disabilities, and simplified user interfaces. Language support broadens participation, helping to bridge divides caused by linguistic differences. By proactively designing for diversity and difference, communities can dismantle exclusionary patterns and invite richer, more equitable engagement.

Combating abuse and exclusion is undeniably complex,

requiring layered, thoughtful responses grounded in respect for human dignity. It demands vigilance against overt harms and subtle biases alike, harnessing the strengths of technology, community action, and empathetic governance. Ultimately, creating safer, more inclusive spaces is an ongoing collective project—one that strives to ensure every voice can be heard without fear, every identity recognized without prejudice, and every community a place of genuine belonging.

7.4 Freedom of Expression versus Harm

Freedom of expression, long hailed as a cornerstone of democracy, embodies the right to articulate ideas, opinions, and information without undue restraint. Traditionally enshrined as protection from government censorship, its digital manifestation now extends to the vast, unruly expanse of online platforms. Here, the simplicity of "speak freely" is complicated by the sheer scale of voices, the speed of communication, and the diversity of communities. This creates a pressing question: how do we preserve the essence of free speech while responsibly mitigating harm, misinformation, and abusive content that proliferate in these virtual spaces?

At its core, freedom of expression in online realms means users should be able to share thoughts without fear of arbitrary suppression. However, this right is not absolute. It has always carried intrinsic limits designed to balance individual liberty with collective well-being. Even classic legal frameworks acknowledge exceptions: speech that incites violence, defames others, or constitutes hate propaganda can be restricted. In digital environments—where harmful content can replicate, amplify, and target vulnerable groups instantly—these boundaries become more critical and, yet, more fluid.

Platforms find themselves navigating complex ethical tradeoffs. On one hand, openness fuels innovation, democratic deliberation, and social connection. On the other, unchecked expression can foster hostility, spread falsehoods, invade privacy, or degrade the very spaces meant for exchange. Privacy and safety, distinct but intertwined, often clash with the desire for open discourse. Striking a balance requires platforms to weigh competing values: promoting a vibrant public square while safeguarding users from harm. This ethical negotiation constitutes the invisible framework directing content moderation policies.

Determining what counts as harmful content versus protected speech hinges on careful harm thresholds. Typically, speech causing direct, tangible harm—such as incitement to violence, targeted harassment, or credible threats—falls outside the protective ambit. Ambiguities arise with speech that offends or discomforts but does not inflict measurable damage. Here, platforms often exercise discretion, informed by legal standards, community norms, and the evolving understanding of harm in digital contexts. Criteria include the severity, intent, immediacy, and likelihood of harm, underscoring that not all offensive or controversial speech warrants removal.

Contextual moderation emerges as a crucial tool in these delicate decisions. Content cannot be evaluated in isolation from its social, cultural, or conversational setting. For example, a statement deemed provocative in one setting might be scholarly critique in another, or satire in yet another. Intent—whether to inform, criticize, troll, or threaten—also colors interpretation, as does audience. Protective measures might differ if the speech targets vulnerable populations or occurs within closed groups versus public forums. By incorporating context, moderation endeavors to respect nuance and avoid mechanistic blanket bans, though this also increases complexity and potential inconsistency.

Platforms formalize their approach through hate speech policies, which articulate definitions, prohibited behaviors, and enforcement thresholds. Such policies usually prohibit language inciting discrimination or violence based on race, ethnicity, religion, gender, sexuality, or other identity markers. Enforcement often adopts graduated responses: content removal, warnings, account suspension, or permanent bans. To maintain fairness, many platforms incorporate appeals processes allowing users to contest decisions. These policies must contend with linguistic subtleties, cultural variability, and the challenge of distinguishing hate speech from legitimate dissent or criticism.

Misinformation, especially when it endangers public health or democratic integrity, poses another distinct challenge. Fact-checking initiatives, partnerships with independent reviewers, and algorithmic labeling help flag disputed claims. Platforms may downrank misleading content, reducing its visibility without outright removal, thereby balancing correction with free expression. However, the definition of misinformation is itself contested territory, often reflecting evolving scientific consensus or political fault lines. Controls must avoid overreach while curtailing viral falsehoods that can amplify real-world harm.

This delicate dance inevitably risks censorship overreach, bias, and chilling effects on discourse. Overzealous or opaque moderation can stifle dissent, marginalize minority views, or silence legitimate debates. Algorithmic moderation introduces concerns about embedded biases and errors magnified at scale.

Such risks call for vigilance to prevent the suppression of lawful, valuable speech under the guise of moderation, preserving the diversity and dynamism essential to open platforms.

Transparency plays an essential role in maintaining trust amid these tensions. Public transparency reports sharing statistics on removed content, account suspensions, and policy enforcement enable users to grasp how moderation functions in practice. Moderation logs and user notifications also foster accountability, informing individuals why their content was removed or restricted. This openness helps demystify decisions, reduce perceptions of arbitrariness, and invite constructive engagement with platform governance.

Ensuring users have avenues of recourse further anchors respect for rights. Appeals processes provide users the chance to challenge moderation actions, thereby reinforcing procedural fairness. Outcome reporting— detailing appeal success rates and reasoning—further illuminates the system's responsiveness and areas for improvement. Such mechanisms embody the principles of due process in digital speech governance, balancing enforcement with user empowerment.

Examining major platforms offers revealing case studies in these tradeoffs. Facebook's complex, evolving community standards exemplify attempts to balance openness with safety, deploying extensive content reviewers, AI systems, and appeals processes. Twitter's evolving policies on harassment and misinformation reflect challenges in applying consistent enforcement amid diverse political pressures. Both platforms' experiences demonstrate that perfect balance is elusive, requiring continuous iteration, stakeholder dialogue, and humility.

Ultimately, the interplay between freedom of expression and harm prevention in online spaces is less a zero-sum contest than a dynamic equilibrium. It demands ongoing negotiation, attuned to evolving social values, technological affordances, and empirical understanding of harm. By grounding policies in clear principles, nuanced context, and transparent processes, platforms strive to foster online environments where speech remains vibrant yet responsible—a public square where ideas flourish without inflicting undue damage.

7.5 Legal Aspects and Platform Liability

The internet, with its unprecedented capacity for expression and connection, poses a profound legal challenge: how should the law treat platforms that host user-generated content? At the heart of this question lies a fundamental distinction between the platform as a mere conduit and the individual user as the originator of speech. Legislators and courts have wrestled with this difference, mindful that holding platforms liable for everything posted would stifle innovation and communication, while granting them unfettered immunity risks enabling harm and abuse.

Traditionally, the law distinguishes platforms from individual users by recognizing that platforms often do not create or edit the content they host; they merely provide the infrastructure. This conceptual separation underpins various legal protections and responsibilities. Platforms are generally not treated as publishers or speakers for the content provided by third parties. Instead, they occupy a middle ground—as facilitators whose liability is limited so long as they act responsibly in response to problematic content. This balancing act shapes the regulatory landscape worldwide.

In the United States, Section 230 of the Communications Decency Act stands as the cornerstone of platform immunity. Enacted in 1996, Section 230 famously states that platforms "shall not be treated as the publisher or speaker" of third-party content. This legal safe harbor shields platforms from the vast majority of lawsuits arising from what users post, enabling the explosive growth of social media, forums, and other interactive services. The law encourages platforms to moderate content in good faith without fear of being deemed liable for making editorial decisions, a protection that remains vital to online discourse.

Yet, Section 230's broad immunity has generated controversy. Critics argue that it allows platforms to evade responsibility for harmful content, from misinformation to hate speech, while others worry that weakening these protections could force platforms into over-censorship to avoid liability. The debate continues as lawmakers consider reforms aiming to balance accountability with free expression and innovation.

Across the Atlantic, the European Union takes a different approach, especially in data protection. The General Data Protection Regulation (GDPR), implemented in 2018, transformed the obligations of online platforms handling personal data. Unlike Section 230's focus on speech, the GDPR centers on users' privacy rights, imposing strict rules on data collection, processing, and transfer. Platforms must obtain clear consent, enable user control, and ensure data security under threat of hefty fines reaching millions of euros.

GDPR's ripple effects extend beyond Europe; many global platforms have adapted their practices worldwide to comply. Its emphasis on transparency and user empowerment changes how platforms design services and how users perceive data governance. Importantly, GDPR also pressures platforms to be more accountable not just for what users say, but for how users' digital footprints are managed and protected.

When it comes to managing defamatory or unlawful speech, platforms face thorny legal questions. Defamation—the act of damaging someone's reputation by false statements—remains actionable even online. However, since platforms do not originate content, liability often hinges on whether they promptly and effectively remove offending material once notified. Many jurisdictions employ notice-and-takedown procedures that balance freedom of expression with individual rights. A user claiming defamation typically notifies the platform, which then must evaluate and potentially take down the content to avoid liability.

This procedure, while conceptually straightforward, is frequently fraught with complexity. There is a delicate tension between preventing abuse of takedown requests (which may be used to silence legitimate speech) and protecting victims from harm. Platforms thus develop policies and mechanisms to review complaints prudently, often supplemented by appeals processes to ensure fairness and transparency.

Intellectual property rights present another key frontier. Under laws like the United States' Digital Millennium Copyright Act (DMCA), platforms benefit from safe harbor provisions that protect them from liability if they promptly remove copyrighted materials upon receiving valid takedown notices. The DMCA's notice-and-takedown mechanism empowers copyright holders but also raises concerns regarding overreach or improper censorship.

Importantly, the DMCA includes a counter-notice proce-dure allowing users to contest removals, promoting due process amid the often-opaque world of digital rights enforcement. Platforms typically maintain teams and au-tomated systems to handle millions of requests, striking a challenging balance between protecting rights holders and preserving legitimate content.

Beyond external regulations, platforms also rely on contracts with users—terms of service (ToS)—to set the rules of engagement. These agreements delineate user rights, platform responsibilities, and dispute resolution mechanisms, commonly featuring arbitration clauses that restrict legal action to private proceedings. While ToS provide legal clarity, their complexity and length often mean users accept them without full understanding, leading to questions about informed consent and fairness.

Courts generally uphold ToS as contracts, granting platforms considerable latitude to enforce community standards, suspend accounts, or terminate services. However, tensions arise when platform policies intersect with fundamental rights, such as expression or privacy, prompting ongoing debate about the appropriate limits of contractual authority in digital spaces.

Data breaches starkly reveal the stakes of platform liability and data protection. When user data is exposed through hacks or accidental leaks, platforms face not only reputational damage but regulatory penalties and mandatory notification duties. Laws worldwide increasingly require prompt disclosure to affected individuals and authorities, fostering transparency and enabling users to take protective measures.

For example, under the GDPR, data breaches that risk user rights must be reported within 72 hours, with failures incurring fines proportional to a platform's global revenue. Similarly, in the United States, state laws vary but often mandate disclosure to consumers and may impose additional security requirements. These regulations incentivize platforms to invest heavily in cybersecurity and breach preparedness, recognizing that safeguarding data is now a cornerstone of platform trustworthiness and legal compliance.

The global nature of the internet complicates regulation due to cross-border jurisdiction issues. Platforms operating internationally must navigate the often conflicting laws of multiple countries, each with their own standards for speech, privacy, intellectual property, and liability. For instance, speech permissible in one nation might be illegal in another; data protection regimes vary widely; and enforcement agencies may demand content removals or user data that clash with other jurisdictions' laws.

Resolving these conflicts demands nuanced legal frameworks, bilateral agreements, or multilateral treaties. Platforms sometimes geo-block content or impose local compliance measures to address jurisdictional challenges, yet the fundamental tension between national sovereignty and the borderless internet remains unresolved, fueling calls for harmonized global norms or flexible regulatory models.

Enforcement itself presents thorny challenges. Anonymity and encryption technologies protect user privacy and freedom but complicate investigations into illegal activities or harmful speech. Authorities face difficulties identifying perpetrators, while due process must be balanced against urgent demands for action. Platforms may be pressured to weaken encryption or provide backdoors, sparking fierce debates on security versus surveillance.

207

Moreover, investigating online harm risks overreach, censorship, or AI-driven errors that remove innocent content. These enforcement dilemmas reveal the complex interplay among law, technology, and human rights in the digital age, underscoring the need for transparent accountability mechanisms and ongoing dialogue among stakeholders.

Looking ahead, new regulatory initiatives seek to recalibrate platform responsibility. The European Union's Digital Services Act (DSA), set to take effect soon, exemplifies this trend by imposing clearer obligations for moderating content, transparency reporting, and risk assessment on very large platforms. It aims to harmonize rules across member states while safeguarding fundamental rights and fostering innovation.

The DSA and similar proposals worldwide signal a shift from immunity toward conditional responsibility, where platforms actively demonstrate compliance without becoming arbiters of truth or enforcers of political will. This evolving legal landscape invites platforms, users, regulators, and civil society to rethink the governance of online spaces in ways that promote safety, fairness, and openness.

In sum, the legal aspects of platform liability unfold as a dynamic, multidimensional puzzle. The law strives to recognize platforms' unique role—as intermediaries and enablers—while protecting users' rights and societal interests. Navigating this regulatory terrain requires continuous adaptation, creative solutions, and a shared commitment to balancing innovation, responsibility, and fundamental freedoms in the ever-changing digital ecosystem.

7.6 Design for Equity and Inclusion

At the heart of creating vibrant virtual communities lies a fundamental commitment to *fairness*—a commitment that extends beyond mere equality. Equality, simply put, means giving everyone the same resources or opportunities. But equity digs deeper: it calls for recognizing differences in needs, circumstances, and histories, and then tailoring support to ensure everyone has a genuine chance to participate and thrive. Imagine a digital platform that offers the same font size and color contrast to all users. While this might seem equal, it fails those with visual impairments who require larger text or higher contrast. Designing for equity means adapting such features to meet diverse needs, not merely distributing the same tools to all.

This distinction is crucial when crafting virtual spaces meant to bring together people from varied backgrounds, capabilities, and identities. Equality assumes a level playing field, while equity acknowledges that some start with more hurdles than others. This is why designers, especially those shaping online communities, must prioritize practices that are *fair* and *accessible*, rather than just uniform.

Inclusive design principles offer a robust framework for this endeavor. Rooted in the belief that good design benefits everyone, these principles emphasize anticipating a wide spectrum of users' needs rather than retrofitting solutions after exclusion is discovered. Frameworks such as the Microsoft Inclusive Design approach advocate for recognizing exclusion, learning from diversity, and solving for one—then many. This means identifying specific challenges faced by individuals or groups (such as limited internet access, disabilities, or linguistic barriers) and designing

209

features that can flexibly accommodate these variations. For example, providing text alternatives for images, customizable user interface settings, and multilingual support positions a platform to serve users more equitably from the outset.

Yet, inclusive design demands more than intuition; it must confront an often invisible adversary—algorithmic bias. Virtual communities increasingly rely on algorithms that shape user experience: recommending content, filtering conversations, or moderating behavior. These algorithms, however, are susceptible to inheriting and amplifying biases embedded in their training data or design. For instance, if a moderation algorithm disproportionately flags language used by marginalized groups based on biased data, those users may feel censored or unwelcome. Mitigating such bias requires vigilance: continuous testing with diverse user sets, transparency around decision rules, and introducing fairness constraints to keep algorithms aligned with inclusive values.

Accessibility standards provide critical technical footholds to ensure platforms are usable by everyone, including people with disabilities. The Web Content Accessibility Guidelines (WCAG), developed by the World Wide Web Consortium (W3C), specify criteria for perceivable, operable, understandable, and robust content. Compliance with WCAG ensures, for example, that screen readers can interpret site elements, keyboard navigation is fully supported, and color contrasts meet minimum thresholds. Beyond mere compliance, designing with accessibility in mind fosters innovation— voice commands, flexible layouts, and alternative input methods often emerge from these considerations, improving the experience for all users.

Representation also plays a vital role in fostering inclusion. Visual and social cues embedded in avatars, pronoun options, and imagery send powerful signals about who belongs in a community. Offering diverse avatar choices that reflect a broad range of ethnicities, gender expressions, and abilities empowers users to see themselves reflected and valued. Allowing custom or nonbinary pronouns supports identity authenticity, which in turn cultivates trust and respect. Moreover, using culturally sensitive imagery and avoiding stereotypes helps prevent alienation and fragmentation that can fray the social fabric of virtual spaces.

To truly design for equity and inclusion, it is paramount to engage in community consultation and participatory design. Co-creating platforms with underrepresented groups is the antidote to assumptions that often overlook nuanced challenges. When users become partners rather than mere subjects, the resulting designs resonate authentically with lived experiences. For example, involving Deaf community members in testing chat features can reveal subtleties in transcription quality or timing that might otherwise be missed. This collaborative approach strengthens trust, surfaces novel ideas, and yields solutions rooted in empathy.

Cultural sensitivity extends beyond mere representation to encompass language, symbols, and social norms embedded in community design. Words carry immense power: terms that seem neutral in one culture might be offensive or exclusionary in another. Iconography, color choices, and interaction norms must be carefully vetted with cultural awareness to avoid unintended marginalization. For instance, a hand gesture used as a friendly greeting in one region may be inappropriate elsewhere. Incorporating multilingual support and allowing customization of cultural settings fosters environments where global participants feel respected and at ease.

Measuring fairness and inclusion remains an ongoing challenge, but applying both quantitative and qualitative metrics can illuminate progress and pitfalls. Quantitative fairness metrics might analyze participation rates across demographic groups, the diversity of content creators, or discrepancies in moderation outcomes. Qualitative measures—such as user satisfaction surveys, focus groups, and ethnographic studies—capture nuanced experiences that numbers alone cannot. Together, these assessments form a feedback loop critical to uncovering hidden biases and ensuring equitable treatment.

Sustaining equity is not a "design-and-forget" task; it requires continuous improvement. Rigorous audit cycles, regular user feedback loops, and timely policy reviews are essential to adapting to evolving community dynamics. For instance, as new accessibility technologies emerge or privacy concerns rise, platforms must revisit their guidelines and interfaces to stay relevant and inclusive. Proactively addressing emerging issues rather than reacting post-hoc nurtures vibrant, resilient virtual communities where everyone can contribute fully.

Finally, governance structures play an instrumental role in embedding inclusion into the fabric of virtual communities. Establishing diversity councils, ethics boards, or inclusion committees formalizes accountability and expertise in decision-making. Transparency in governance fosters trust: when users know that policies and platform changes are informed by diverse voices and ethical deliberation, engagement deepens. Such bodies can champion equitable practices, adjudicate conflicts with empathy, and guide long-term visions that honor inclusion as a non-negotiable principle.

Designing for equity and inclusion is both an art

and a science—not a one-off checklist but a dynamic commitment. It requires blending rigorous frameworks with genuine human empathy, robust technical standards with cultural agility, and constant vigilance against bias. When virtual communities embrace these principles, they transform from mere networks into welcoming spaces where the richness of human diversity flourishes, unlocking untapped potential and forging connections that transcend physical boundaries.

Chapter 8

The Future of Virtual Communities

*This chapter peers beyond today's digital gatherings to antici-
pate the technologies, social dynamics, and best practices that
will shape tomorrow's virtual communities. We explore immersive 3D worlds and the metaverse, AI-driven management
tools, and decentralized governance models. We then examine how communities can sustain themselves over time, translate online bonds into real-world impact, and uphold member
safety and wellbeing in an evolving digital landscape.*

8.1 Virtual Reality, Metaverses, and Immersive Worlds

The concept of the *metaverse* has shifted from speculative
fiction to an emerging reality: a shared, persistent,
three-dimensional virtual environment where people
gather not only for entertainment but also for social
interaction, work, and commerce. Unlike isolated
virtual experiences of the past, these metaverses aim to
create ongoing worlds that exist independently of any
individual user's presence. They weave together the
immersive capabilities of virtual and augmented reality
(VR/AR), the social dynamics of human connection,
and the complexity of digital economies into a cohesive,

evolving digital fabric.

At its core, the metaverse is a digital space that feels as tangible as physical reality. To enter and engage meaningfully, users often employ VR technologies centered around head-mounted displays (HMDs) that provide stereoscopic visuals and wide fields of view. Complementing this visual immersion are spatial audio systems, which render sound with directional accuracy, helping users locate voices and environmental cues naturally within the 3D space. Touch and interaction go beyond sight and sound through haptic feedback devices—gloves, suits, or controllers that simulate texture, resistance, or impact—bridging the divide between digital and physical sensations. These technologies converge with mixed reality interfaces, blending virtual objects seamlessly into a user's actual surroundings or overlaying information in the real world, further enriching the experiential depth.

Identity within these worlds is realized through *avatars*: customizable digital embodiments that often range from highly realistic human likenesses to fantastical creations. Avatars serve as both social masks and channels of self-expression, enabling users to convey personality traits, cultural affiliations, or simply experiment with new identities. This embodiment fosters a sense of presence—a psychological feeling of "being there" inside the metaverse—which is pivotal for meaningful interaction. Personalization tools let users adjust appearance, gestures, and animations, supporting diverse modes of communication and emotional nuance.

Crucially, social interaction in these immersive worlds extends beyond text and voice chat familiar from traditional internet platforms. Spatial proximity in the virtual space matters: avatars that stand close can hear each other's voices more clearly, fostering natural conversational dynamics. Gestures, head nods, and eye contact, captured either through motion tracking or user input, enrich dialogue with bodily expression, emulating the subtlety of face-to-face encounters. Group activities—from casual meetups to collaborative projects—benefit from this spatialized communication, enabling emergent social phenomena such as shared attention and group cohesion, essential for any thriving community.

Behind these dynamic spaces lie systems of governance designed to maintain order while encouraging creativity and free expression. Moderation in the metaverse combines automated filters, community-elected stewards, and platform rules to address toxicity, harassment, or fraud. Rule-setting reflects a balance between decentralization—where users and developers negotiate norms—and centralized interventions required to enforce safety. Dispute resolution mechanisms increasingly rely on transparent protocols, sometimes inspired by blockchain smart contracts, to adjudicate conflicts fairly and swiftly without disrupting the persistent nature of the world.

Economic activity in metaverses is no mere backdrop but a central pillar supporting sustainability and innovation. Here, virtual land parcels are bought, sold, and developed much like in the physical world, creating digital real estate markets that command real money. Non-fungible tokens (NFTs) grant provable ownership of unique digital assets—ranging from wearable avatar items to artworks and event tickets—empowering creators and collectors alike. In-world cryptocurrencies facilitate transactions that can convert seamlessly to fiat currency, blurring the boundary between digital and physical economies. This growing ecosystem drives entrepreneurship and provides avenues for users to monetize skills, ideas, and social capital in ways previously impossible.

Yet, the promise of a unified metaverse faces significant *interoperability* hurdles. Present-day platforms operate largely in silos, each with distinct standards for avatars, assets, and environmental data. Moving your virtual clothing or identity from one metaverse to another remains cumbersome, if not impossible. Achieving true cross-platform compatibility demands not only technological solutions—open protocols and shared frameworks—but also collaboration among competing corporate and community stakeholders, all while navigating intellectual property rights and security concerns. Without resolving these challenges, the vision of a seamless interconnected metaverse risks fragmentation into isolated digital islands.

Accessibility is another frontier critical to the metaverse's inclusivity and widespread adoption. VR hardware, despite falling prices, still represents a financial barrier for many potential users; high-performance devices and peripherals can be cost-prohibitive. Moreover, the immersive nature of VR can cause motion sickness or fatigue for some, necessitating both technological improvements like lower latency displays and software design that minimizes discomfort. In addition, inclusive design practices seek to accommodate diverse abilities by incorporating customizable control schemes, captions, and alternative sensory modalities, ensuring that these immersive worlds are welcoming environments rather than exclusive clubs.

Despite these nascent challenges, early deployments of metaverse platforms reveal a rich variety of use cases that hint at a future deeply intertwined with daily life. Virtual conferences have moved beyond video calls, offering attendees spatial audio rooms, customizable environments, and spontaneous encounters that echo physical conferences' serendipitous moments. Training simulations in fields such as medicine, aviation, and manufacturing leverage VR's immersive qualities to provide safe, realistic practice without real-world risks or expenses. Social hubs host concerts, art galleries, and gaming events that draw global audiences, unbounded by geography or venue capacities, fostering new forms of cultural participation and community building.

Looking ahead, the trajectory of metaverses involves the interplay of emerging technologies and human creativity. Artificial intelligence promises to populate these worlds with responsive, believable non-player characters and to assist in content generation, automating the expansion and personalization of environments. Advances in mixed reality will blend the physical and digital so seamlessly that our everyday surroundings become canvases for interactive narratives and collaborative workspaces. Ultimately, the metaverse may evolve into a platform for amplified human-computer co-presence, where the boundary between digital and physical selves grows porous, expanding our capacities for communication, creativity, and commerce in ways still unfolding.

The metaverse's unfolding story is not merely about technology but about how we adapt notions of community, identity, economy, and space in a digital age. As persistent, immersive virtual worlds gain prominence, they challenge us to rethink what it means to be present, to belong, and to value experience in the age of ubiquitous digital connectivity.

8.2 Artificial Intelligence in Community Management

The rise of virtual communities—from sprawling social networks to niche forums—has transformed how people connect, share, and collaborate. Managing these bustling digital spaces is no trivial matter: moderators face the daunting task of fostering engagement, curbing harmful behavior, and supporting members' needs, all while preserving a sense of community spirit. Enter artificial intelligence (AI) and machine learning (ML), powerful tools that extend human capabilities by automating routine tasks, sharpening insights, and personalizing experiences. By examining how AI functions within community management, we gain insight into a new era where humans and machines co-create healthier and more vibrant online ecosystems.

At its core, AI is the endeavor to endow computers with the ability to perform tasks that typically require human intelligence—such as understanding language, recognizing patterns, or making decisions. Machine learning, a subset of AI, enables systems to learn from data and improve over time without being explicitly programmed for every scenario. In community management, these technologies serve to relieve humans of repetitive and time-sensitive duties: flagging inappropriate content, guiding newcomers, tailoring content feeds, and anticipating emerging issues. This automation enhances efficiency, but it also challenges us to balance efficacy with ethics and transparency.

One of the earliest and most visible applications of AI in virtual communities is automated moderation. Content-scanning bots patrol forums, chat rooms, and comment sections, using natural language processing and pattern recognition to identify spam, hate speech, or other policy violations. These tools operate at a scale impossible for human moderators alone, swiftly removing harmful posts or flagging them for review. Toxicity detection algorithms analyze not just explicit keywords but also nuanced cues like sarcasm or context. However, the technology is not infallible. False positives—where benign content is misclassified—and false negatives—where harmful content slips through— remain persistent challenges. For example, slang or cultural references may confound the bots, resulting in overzealous censorship or overlooked abuse. As a result, automated moderation systems often work best when paired with human judgment, forming a hybrid defense that balances speed with discretion.

Complementing moderation are AI-powered chatbots and virtual assistants, which have become adept conversational partners within communities. These agents handle routine inquiries—such as *How do I reset my password?* or *Where can I find the community guidelines?*—freeing human moderators to focus on complex interpersonal issues. More sophisticated bots guide newcomers through onboarding processes, introduce platform features, or triage member requests, responding instantly 24/7. By mimicking natural conversation, these assistants reduce friction, help members feel welcomed, and maintain continuous engagement even outside business hours. Such agents demonstrate how AI can enhance the sense of belonging while streamlining support operations.

Personalization stands as a pillar of modern digital experience, and AI-driven recommendation engines lie behind the tailored feeds that keep users scrolling and interacting. These algorithms analyze past activity— likes, comments, shares—along with community-wide trends to prioritize the most relevant content for each member. Techniques like collaborative filtering identify users with similar interests and suggest content popular within those clusters, while relevance ranking algorithms weigh factors such as recency and user preferences. Personalization not only elevates user satisfaction by surfacing meaningful discussions but also promotes diverse participation by connecting individuals to corners of the community they might not discover on their own. Yet, there is a delicate balance here: algorithms must avoid creating echo chambers or reinforcing biases while still providing a satisfying, customized experience.

The global and fast-moving nature of virtual communities demands tools that transcend language and volume barriers. Automated summarization condenses lengthy threads or meeting transcripts into digestible nuggets, helping members catch up without wading through extensive logs. Simultaneously, AI-driven translation enables multilingual communities to communicate fluidly, breaking down linguistic silos and fostering cross-cultural exchange. These technologies rely on advances in natural language understanding that capture context, tone, and nuance—no small feat given the complexity of human discourse. By making information accessible and inclusive, summarization and translation play key roles in sustaining large-scale, diverse communities.

Beyond content moderation and personalization, AI systems provide dynamic insights into the community's emotional pulse and evolving interests through sentiment and trend analysis. By scanning posts, comments, and reactions in real time, these tools track the overall mood, detect spikes in frustration or excitement, and pinpoint emergent topics garnering attention. For community managers, such intelligence serves as an early warning system and a source of strategic guidance—for example, signaling when a policy change provokes unrest or when a new initiative captures enthusiasm. This capability transforms raw data into actionable understanding, enabling communities to respond with empathy and agility.

A natural extension of analytical AI is predictive intervention, where machine learning models forecast potential conflicts, user churn, or spikes in support needs before they fully materialize. By scrutinizing patterns in member behavior, message tone, and participation frequency, these systems can alert moderators to users at risk of disengagement or disputes likely to escalate. Armed with such foresight, community leaders can proactively reach out, mediate tensions, or tailor outreach efforts to retain membership and preserve harmony. While predictive models do not claim perfect clairvoyance, they exemplify the promise of anticipatory governance—shifting from reactive crisis management to preventive care.

Despite these advancements, AI rarely operates in isolation within communities; its greatest strength lies in collaboration with human actors. Effective workflows embed AI as a supportive ally, where algorithms flag content but humans confirm, where chatbots handle routine queries but escalate nuanced issues, and where AI-generated summaries supplement rather than replace human summaries. This symbiosis respects the limitations of automation—context, empathy, ethical judgment—and leverages human creativity and wisdom. Rather than replacing moderators, AI frees them to focus on strategic tasks, community building, and nuanced conflict resolution. The resulting partnership enhances safety, responsiveness, and inclusivity without sacrificing the human warmth essential to vibrant communities.

However, the integration of AI carries ethical considerations that demand scrutiny. Automated decisions about content removal, user ranking, or intervention carry risks of bias—stemming from skewed training data or opaque algorithms—that may inadvertently marginalize voices or perpetuate stereotypes. Transparency about how AI is used and clear communication with community members fosters trust and accountability. Informed consent regarding data collection and algorithmic filtering respects users' autonomy and privacy. Moreover, ongoing monitoring and inclusive design practices help mitigate unintended harms and ensure AI tools serve the community's values rather than undermine them. Ethical AI in community management requires vigilance as much as technological sophistication.

Looking ahead, the role of AI in community management is poised to deepen through innovations like self-learning communities and autonomous governance agents. Imagine virtual spaces that not only adapt to user behavior but evolve their own rules and norms through collective input facilitated by AI mediators. Autonomous agents could monitor fairness, moderate disputes impartially, and suggest improvements dynamically, essentially acting as digital stewards. These developments promise more scalable, resilient, and democratic communities—though they also provoke questions about control, accountability, and the nature of human agency online. As AI capabilities grow, the challenge will be to harness their potential while preserving the genuine human connections at the heart of every community.

Artificial intelligence thus enriches community management by augmenting human efforts across moderation, personalization, support, and strategic foresight. It offers tools to tame complexity, enhance engagement, and promote inclusiveness at scales unimaginable just decades ago. Yet these advances flourish only when guided by ethical principles and in tight partnership with the nuanced judgment and care that define community life. The future of virtual communities will be shaped not by technology alone, but by the thoughtful integration of AI into the human endeavor of building and sustaining meaningful connections.

8.3 Decentralization and Blockchain-Based Communities

The notion of decentralization fundamentally challenges the traditional way we structure communities, ownership, and governance by redistributing power from a central authority into the hands of many. Whereas centralized platforms are organized around proprietary control—think of social media giants or corporate-owned marketplaces—decentralized architectures entrust their participants with direct decision-making and value sharing. This shift is not merely a change in technology but a reimagining of social contracts, enabled primarily by blockchain innovations such as Decentralized Autonomous Organizations (DAOs), tokens, and smart contracts.

At the heart of blockchain-based communities lies a distributed ledger—a secure, transparent, and immutable record maintained collectively by network participants rather than a single entity. This ledger is governed by consensus algorithms that ensure agreement on the recorded data without requiring trust in a centralized operator. Public blockchains, like Ethereum, offer open participation and full visibility of transactions, fostering transparency and trustworthiness, while private or permissioned chains restrict access, prioritizing privacy and control. Together, these structures form the technological bedrock on which new forms of ownership and governance are constructed.

DAOs exemplify how decentralization can reconfigure governance. They are organizations encoded on blockchains, operating through predefined rules embedded in smart contracts—self-executing protocols that automatically enforce terms without intermediaries. Instead of hierarchical management, DAOs distribute decision-making power among stakeholders, often proportionate to governance tokens they hold. These tokens serve as both a measure of ownership and voting weight, enabling on-chain proposal submission, discussion, and resolution without relying on traditional, opaque boardrooms.

For example, *The DAO*, launched in 2016, was among the first attempts to translate organizational governance into programmable form. Although it faced early challenges, it demonstrated the potential of token-based governance where community members collectively decide on funding projects or policies through transparent, verifiable votes. Today, dozens of DAOs oversee everything from decentralized finance platforms to social networks, art collectives, and even charities—all governed through tokenized ownership rather than fixed hierarchies.

Tokens themselves are revolutionary instruments. Beyond representing financial value, tokens can encode varied rights—access to services, voting privileges, or dividend claims—effectively transforming how ownership and incentives intersect. Unlike traditional equity or membership rights, which are often paperbound and limited by geographic or legal restrictions, blockchain tokens are programmable and borderless. This universality makes it possible to design incentive mechanisms that reward participation, contribution, or loyalty in real time and in a transparent manner.

Incentive structures are critical to fostering vibrant decentralized communities. Staking—temporarily locking tokens as a commitment to the network's health—is one such mechanism that aligns individual behavior with collective well-being. Participants who stake tokens might earn rewards for validating transactions or for voting on governance proposals, thereby incentivizing active and responsible involvement. Token-driven incentives transform passive stakeholders into engaged collaborators, a stark contrast to centralized systems where users often lack meaningful influence or transparent feedback loops.

Smart contracts underpin these governance and incentive systems by codifying community rules into code that executes automatically and without bias. These programs can automatically distribute rewards, enforce contribution thresholds, or initiate collective actions like funding disbursements—all transparently and without manual intervention. Importantly, they also allow for upgrade paths, where rules can evolve through agreed-on proposals rather than arbitrary executive decisions, thus embedding adaptability into the community's framework.

This codification raises profound questions about the nature of ownership and control. In blockchain-based communities, ownership is granular and dynamic—reflected in tokens that represent slices of an ecosystem and can be traded or combined to shift influence. Governance emerges from collective consensus rather than fiat decrees, fostering a kind of digital sovereignty where participants' voices matter directly and proportionately. This is a stark departure from centralized governance, which often concentrates power and obfuscates decision-making processes.

Yet decentralization also invites complexity, especially when balancing transparency with privacy. Public ledgers provide openness that builds trust but can expose sensitive user information or strategic decisions. Emerging privacy-preserving technologies seek to mediate this tension—such as zero-knowledge proofs or selective disclosure credentials—that allow verification without revealing unnecessary data. Communities must negotiate these privacy-transparency trade-offs according to their values and needs, further underscoring that decentralization is as much a social design challenge as a technical one.

The landscape of decentralized communities also contends with scalability and security challenges. Consensus algorithms, while critical for trust, often have throughput limitations; governance systems may be vulnerable to attacks like vote-buying or collusion; and network forks can create fragmentation. Despite these constraints, ongoing innovation—layer-two scaling solutions, hybrid governance models combining on-chain and off-chain elements, and evolving regulatory frameworks—promises to refine the balance between decentralization's ideals and operational realities.

Practical examples illuminate these concepts vividly. *Aragon* and *MolochDAO* have developed frameworks enabling users to create and manage DAOs with relatively low friction, democratizing access to collective governance tools. Decentralized social networks like *Lens Protocol* aim to replace centralized platforms by giving users control over their content and interactions, often rewarded through native tokens. Beyond purely digital domains, tokenized real estate, art, and even scientific research projects show how blockchain communities can redefine ownership in the physical world.

As we look forward, the boundaries between blockchain-enabled decentralization and traditional institutions may blur. Hybrid models blending on-chain transparency with off-chain expertise and enforcement could address the nuanced demands of complex governance, making decentralization more practical and inclusive. Likewise, regulatory frameworks will likely evolve to protect participants without stifling innovation, fostering an ecosystem where decentralized communities can coexist alongside established entities.

Decentralization and blockchain-based communities promise a paradigm where governance, ownership, and incentives become more democratic, transparent, and aligned with participant interests. While the journey toward fully decentralized systems is ongoing and fraught with challenges, the ongoing innovations in DAOs, tokens, and smart contracts offer glimpses of futures where collective agency is encoded into the very fabric of the digital commons, reshaping how we imagine cooperation in the networked age.

8.4 Sustainability and Lifespan of Online Groups

Online communities, like living organisms, move through distinct phases that shape their existence and ultimate fate. Understanding these stages—birth, growth, maturity, decline, and potential renewal—is essential to nurturing vibrant digital ecosystems that endure beyond fleeting trends.

At inception, a community is often a tight-knit assembly of passionate individuals rallying around a shared interest or goal. This *birth* phase is marked by enthusiasm and rapid idea exchange, but also fragility, as early structures and norms are fluid and informal. Success here hinges on attracting initial members who contribute actively and define the community's identity.

As participation grows, the community enters the *growth* stage. New memberships swell, discussions deepen, and roles begin to crystallize. Administrators and moderators emerge to steward content and social behavior. However, unchecked expansion risks diluting focus or overwhelming governance, making intentional design and clear guidelines crucial.

When a community reaches *maturity*, it displays stability with well-established routines, rituals, and hierarchies. Engagement patterns flatten into predictable rhythms, and a core membership base drives discussions. This stage's challenge is maintaining vitality and relevance rather than simply sustaining numbers. Without adaptation, maturity can stagnate, setting the stage for *decline*.

Decline often manifests as dwindling participation, eroding content quality, and diminished newcomer attraction. Causes range from competition, shifts in member interests, platform policy changes, or internal conflicts. Recognizing early warning signs—such as decreased daily active user ratios or slowing response times—is vital for intervention.

Not all communities fade irreversibly. Some successfully navigate *renewal* by reinventing themselves through rebranding, mission realignment, or evolving norms. Renewal injects fresh energy while honoring foundational values, demonstrating that adaptability is key to longevity.

Measuring a community's health involves more than raw membership figures. Metrics such as the ratio of daily active users (DAU) to monthly active users (MAU) provide insight into habitual engagement. A high DAU/MAU ratio suggests that members return frequently, indicating a vibrant, sticky environment. Alongside this, *retention curves* track the percentage of newcomers who remain active over time, illuminating onboarding effectiveness. The depth of engagement—how extensively members participate in discussions, content creation, or moderation—is another vital indicator. Finally, response times matter: communities that promptly address posts and queries foster a sense of inclusiveness and responsiveness, reinforcing member commitment.

Behind every thriving community lies intentional leadership nurturing its ecosystem. Long-term sustainability depends on avoiding a single-point failure: when too much responsibility or authority rests on one or a few individuals, what happens if they burn out or leave? Sustainable leadership models promote *succession* through mentoring newcomers into roles of responsibility and systematically rotating duties to prevent fatigue. Empowering diverse leaders not only distributes workload but also reflects the community's evolving composition, enriching decision-making and conflict resolution.

Financial and resource strategies also empower longevity. Online communities thrive on various support models:

- *Donations* from engaged members, fostering a sense of collective ownership.

- *Subscriptions* or premium memberships that offer

added value in exchange for steady revenue.

- Sponsorships from aligned organizations that provide capital but may introduce influence, which must be managed carefully to maintain community autonomy.

- Emerging models such as *token economies* in decentralized platforms, experimenting with incentivizing participation and governance through digital assets.

Each approach has trade-offs, but establishing a transparent, sustainable funding mechanism is a cornerstone of long-term health.

Technical infrastructure, often invisible but foundational, demands continuous attention. Over time, *technical debt* accumulates—think of it as the cost of quick fixes and ad hoc solutions. Left unchecked, this hampers performance, frustrates users, and complicates new feature additions. Proactive management includes periodic code refactoring, where underlying systems are cleaned and optimized; platform migrations to more scalable or secure environments; and feature pruning, which involves retiring underused or obsolete functions to reduce complexity. This upkeep ensures that technology remains an enabler rather than a barrier.

Just as software evolves, so too must community culture. *Cultural renewal* might involve rebranding to appeal to broader or new audiences, shifting mission statements to reflect changing priorities, or revising norms and etiquette to foster inclusiveness and adapt to social trends. Such evolution keeps a community relevant and welcoming without betraying its roots. Importantly, cultural flexibility should be balanced with stability to preserve identity—a delicate dance that requires ongoing dialogue and consensus-building.

Communities, especially those driven by volunteers, must also address the twin perils of conflict and burnout. Interpersonal tensions can escalate quickly in online environments where miscommunication is common. Establishing clear conflict resolution mechanisms, promoting respectful discourse, and providing avenues for mediation can prevent fractures. Equally critical is recognizing volunteer fatigue; active contributors often shoulder disproportionate burdens, risking exhaustion. Encouraging role rotation, offering recognition, and fostering a supportive atmosphere help sustain energy and goodwill.

Forward-thinking communities plan their legacy through *archival and preservation* efforts. Retaining a record of conversations, decisions, and contributions not only documents history but facilitates continuity through leadership changes. Open-sourcing platform code or releasing community guidelines publicly extends impact beyond immediate participants, inviting new collaborators. Archival facilitates reflection on what worked and what didn't, informing future strategies.

The online world constantly shifts under communities' feet. Adapting to *external changes*—be they regulatory updates, evolving platform policies, or technological breakthroughs—is essential. For instance, data privacy laws may compel changes in user management; shifts in dominant social media algorithms can affect visibility and recruitment; emerging communication tools can redefine interaction modes. Resilient communities anticipate these forces and respond proactively rather than reactively, building buffers and diversifying platforms when possible.

Looking ahead, sustainable online communities may embrace *future resilience strategies* that embed adaptability into their DNA. Dynamic governance models enable flexible decision-making responsive to member feedback and changing conditions. Continuous feedback loops collect and act upon community sentiment, preventing stagnation. Some pioneers even explore *community insurance*—mechanisms to safeguard resources or user data against unforeseen disruptions.

Altogether, the sustainability and lifespan of online groups hinge on a delicate balance of structural soundness, cultural vitality, technological upkeep, and adaptive leadership. Like ecosystems that survive through cycles of growth and renewal, digital communities flourish when nurtured with foresight, inclusivity, and openness to change.

8.5 Virtual Communities and Real-World Impact

The boundary between the online and offline worlds has grown increasingly porous, producing what might best be described as an *online–offline continuum*. Rather than existing as separate spheres, our virtual communities and physical lives weave together in intricate hybrid forms. Individuals engage digitally with like-minded groups but often carry those connections into face-to-face encounters, shared projects, and real-world endeavors. This fusion reshapes social dynamics, political action, economic activity, and cultural expression, demonstrating that virtual communities are not mere echoes of offline life—they actively transform it.

At the heart of this continuum are hybrid models

that blend virtual and physical participation. These blendings range from local chapters of global online communities organizing real-world meetups to extensive networks facilitating cross-border collaborations grounded in digital platforms. When members of digital communities convene in person, whether at city parks, rented halls, or international conventions, the abstract ties of online interaction become tangible. These gatherings are more than social occasions; they are laboratories for trust-building, knowledge exchange, and community deepening. They often serve to amplify the value of virtual bonds by adding layers of empathy and understanding that digital text or avatars alone cannot fully convey.

Meetups and conferences illustrate this synergy vividly. Consider how fan conventions like Comic-Con or specialized professional gatherings such as tech developer festivals begin as expressions of online fandoms or career-related forums. They transform virtual enthusiasm into immersive, sensory experiences. Participants exchange ideas, collaborate on projects, and forge personal friendships strengthened by shared physical presence. The proliferation of such events underscores a fundamental truth: online communities seek and thrive on offline embodiment. These moments reinforce collective identity, foster mentorship, and incubate new initiatives that ripple back into digital spaces—making the community an ongoing, cyclical engagement rather than a static forum.

Beyond social bonding, virtual communities increasingly influence civic life and public policy. Digital activism has emerged as a formidable force that transcends geography and traditional power structures, enabling grassroots movements to shape legislation and social norms. Online petitions, coordinated hashtag campaigns, and viral videos mobilize public attention and pressure decision-makers. For example, movements such as #BlackLivesMatter, #MeToo, and climate action coalitions began as digital convenings but quickly transitioned into mass protests, lobbying efforts, and institutional dialogues. These actions illustrate how virtual platforms function as incubators of civic engagement with real consequences—informing public debates, influencing electoral outcomes, and spurring legal reforms. Virtual spaces thus serve both as arenas of community building and as catalysts for structural change in the offline world.

Economic ecosystems have also flourished at the intersection of virtual and physical realms. The rise of creator economies exemplifies how individual talents and passions can monetize through online platforms, transforming leisure into livelihood. Digital marketplaces such as Etsy, Patreon, and OnlyFans allow artists, writers, and content creators to connect directly with global audiences and patrons. Freelancing platforms extend this pattern by coupling digital talent pools with business needs worldwide, effectively erasing traditional employment boundaries. What might begin as virtual collaboration or hobbyist activity often matures into full-fledged economic ventures with tangible offline impacts—ranging from local workshops and product deliveries to international brand partnerships. Community marketplaces fueled by shared values—such as sustainability or ethical sourcing—further demonstrate how virtual networks can give rise to niche industries serving concrete consumer demands.

Education, too, benefits from these virtual-offline synergies. Online groups and forums frequently spawn bootcamps, certification programs, and apprenticeship arrangements that complement or substitute traditional educational institutions. These initiatives capitalize on the mentoring, peer learning, and skill-sharing inherent in virtual communities but formalize them in ways recognized by employers and professional bodies. Coding bootcamps, language exchange groups offering certified proficiency levels, and cooperative workshops in maker spaces illustrate how digital connections can proactively shape individual career trajectories and community capacity. Such educational extensions not only enable flexible, self-directed learning but also democratize access to knowledge and opportunity, especially where formal systems are slow or inaccessible.

Philanthropy and volunteering constitute another vital domain where virtual groups marshal resources and energy for real-world benefit. Crowdsourcing platforms and social media enable rapid coordination of aid efforts, whether in response to natural disasters, public health crises, or humanitarian emergencies. Virtual communities organize fundraising drives, volunteer recruitment, and information dissemination with unprecedented scale and speed. Notable examples include coordinated relief for earthquakes, pandemic support networks delivering supplies to vulnerable populations, and global crowdfunding campaigns addressing causes ranging from education to wildlife conservation. These digitally orchestrated efforts demonstrate how virtual solidarity translates into tangible assistance, often bridging gaps left by traditional institutions.

Cultural production within online communities similarly transcends the digital plane to produce enduring, physical cultural artifacts and shared experiences. Fan fiction, collaborative open-source art, and community-driven media projects challenge

237

conventional notions of authorship, ownership, and creativity. Participants often use digital platforms to co-create stories, music, visual art, and other cultural outputs that inspire offline gatherings, performances, and exhibitions. This participatory culture fosters inclusivity and experimentation, expanding the boundaries of artistic expression. Instances like open-source game development or collectively composed anthologies illustrate how virtual collaboration generates content enriching broader cultural landscapes, fueling innovation within and beyond the community's original digital domain.

Understanding the real-world impact of virtual communities requires more than counting likes or membership numbers; it demands nuanced measures of social value and influence. Tools such as social return on investment (SROI) assess how community activities generate outcomes benefiting individuals, organizations, and society. Qualitative testimonials capture personal transformations and relational depth fostered by online engagement. Meanwhile, impact metrics—ranging from policy changes influenced to funds raised or jobs created—offer concrete data on community effectiveness. Together, these approaches enable stakeholders to appreciate how digital networks catalyze meaningful change offline, guiding both scholarly inquiry and practical strategies for harnessing the power of virtual communities responsibly.

However, the shift from online to offline domains raises important ethical considerations. Privacy, consent, and safety become paramount when virtual interactions materialize in physical spaces. Participants must negotiate boundaries regarding personal information disclosure, unwelcome physical contact, and the potential for harassment or surveillance. Organizers of hybrid events and initiatives must develop clear codes of conduct and protect vulnerable members while fostering inclusivity and openness. These issues underscore the need for on-going vigilance and adaptive governance models to ensure that the benefits of bridging digital and material worlds do not come at the cost of security or dignity.

Looking ahead, the synergies between virtual communities and offline life are poised to deepen through emerging technologies and conceptual innovations. Digital twins of cities—highly detailed virtual replicas—offer new arenas for civic participation, urban planning, and community simulation. Mixed-reality workplaces blend the flexibility of remote collaboration with the richness of co-presence, reshaping how professional and social networks operate. Extended networks may far surpass current online platforms in scope and sophistication, supporting multimodal engagement spanning tactile, auditory, and visual experiences woven between the virtual and physical environment. These future developments invite reflection on how we might cultivate community, identity, and agency in worlds simultaneously real and virtual, individual and collective.

Through these varied dimensions—social, political, economic, educational, philanthropic, cultural, ethical, and technological—virtual communities reveal themselves as dynamic engines of offline transformation. They invite us to rethink the spatial and temporal frameworks of human connection and highlight how digital innovation can enrich rather than diminish our shared reality. Far from being fleeting or illusory, these hybrid communities exert palpable influence on the everyday, shaping societies in ways both subtle and profound.

8.6 Staying Safe and Healthy in a Digital World

Navigating the digital landscape demands more than technical savvy; it requires deliberate care for our wellbeing, security, and sense of community. As our lives increasingly interweave with digital interactions, cultivating habits that protect both our minds and devices becomes essential. Maintaining balance online is not only about what we do but how thoughtfully we engage with technology and with one another.

Fundamental to digital wellbeing is the principle of intentional engagement. Rather than drifting aimlessly through apps and feeds, purposeful use helps preserve mental clarity. Setting boundaries around screen time can prevent exhaustion and reduce the creeping feeling of being constantly "on call." Mindfulness in digital spaces—actively noticing how content affects emotions or attention—grounds us amidst the flood of stimuli. By prioritizing meaningful interactions and conscious breaks, we create space for genuine connection and personal reflection.

Digital safety extends beyond mental habits to the nuts and bolts of cybersecurity. Strong, unique passwords remain a frontline defense against intrusion, especially when combined with two-factor authentication, which adds a second checkpoint to verifying identity. Phishing—those deceptive emails or messages designed to steal information—demands vigilance: pausing to verify suspicious links or unexpected requests can save considerable trouble. Keeping devices updated, running reputable security software, and regularly clearing caches or temporary data form part of essential device hygiene, fortifying defenses against malware and vulnerabilities that threaten personal data.

Speaking of data, privacy hygiene is an increasingly critical area. Practicing data minimization—sharing only the information necessary for a particular service—limits a digital footprint vulnerable to misuse. Pseudonymity, using alternate identities where possible, can safeguard personal details while still enabling participation. At the heart of privacy respect lies informed consent: understanding how platforms collect and use data empowers users to make thoughtful choices. Familiarity with privacy settings and periodic audits of permissions ensure ongoing control, balancing engagement with protection.

Behind every online interaction lurks invisible machinery shaping what we see. Algorithms curate personalized feeds to grab attention, but this tailoring can distort perspectives, amplifying sensational or divisive content. Cultivating algorithmic awareness involves recognizing these filters and seeking diverse information sources to counterbalance potential echo chambers. Transparency—platforms openly describing how personalization works—and user education about feed manipulation elevate digital literacy, nurturing more informed and critical consumption of content.

Staying mentally healthy online also means recognizing when support is needed. Many digital communities now incorporate support groups and crisis resources to assist those facing emotional distress or mental health challenges. Moderated safe spaces offer protections against harassment and harmful content, fostering environments where users feel secure and respected. Normalizing seeking help and maintaining connections within these structures can make a profound difference in navigating digital stressors.

Even with best intentions, disengagement is essential. Digital detox routines—schedules or practices that encourage intentional breaks from screens—help reset focus and reduce burnout. Establishing clear boundaries, such as device-free zones at home or menus that limit app usage, empowers individuals to reclaim control from the demands of persistent connectivity. These intervals of rest nourish creativity and well-being, reminding us that presence in the physical world remains vital.

Physical comfort in a digital age often gets overlooked but matters greatly. Accessible interfaces tailored to diverse abilities ensure broader participation and comfort. Ergonomic hardware—adjustable chairs, wrist supports, or screen filters—reduces strain during extended use. Meanwhile, solo or software-generated break reminders encourage movement and eye rest, staving off fatigue and injury. By integrating accessibility and ergonomics into daily practice, technology becomes a tool that adapts to human needs rather than the other way around.

Inevitable moments of crisis—data loss, security breaches, or harassment—call for resilience and effective recovery. Incident-response protocols help users and communities respond swiftly and decisively, minimizing damage. Maintaining regular data backups guards against catastrophic loss, offering a practical safety net. Crucially, community support networks provide emotional and practical assistance after incidents, reinforcing collective strength. Recovery is not just technical but social: rebuilding trust and reaffirming shared values sustains digital ecosystems through challenges.

Such resilience thrives under community policies that promote safety and respect. Clear guidelines addressing harassment, privacy violations, and consent set shared expectations and empower users to hold one another accountable. Transparent reporting workflows encourage timely action on infractions and support victims. When norms are well communicated and enforced, digital spaces become more welcoming and equitable, underpinning healthier interactions and stronger social bonds.

Finally, the digital terrain is a moving target, requiring lifelong learning to stay secure and well. The rapid evolution of platforms, threats, and norms challenges users to continuously update skills and awareness. Embracing curiosity and adaptability is key to mastering new tools and safeguarding personal boundaries. Educational resources—from tutorials to community workshops—enable ongoing development, fostering confident and informed participation.

Together, these interlocking practices form a blueprint for staying safe and healthy in a digital world. By engaging intentionally, safeguarding security and privacy, supporting mental health, respecting physical comfort, and nurturing community resilience, individuals can not only survive but thrive. The digital realm need not overwhelm; with thoughtful habits and shared commitment, it can enhance our lives while preserving the human spirit at its core.

Chapter 9

Getting Started: Joining and Thriving in Virtual Communities

This practical chapter guides newcomers through each step of finding, joining, and flourishing in online communities. We start by helping you identify the right groups, then cover best practices for introductions and profile setup. Next, we explore relationship-building techniques, meaningful contribution methods, and self-care practices to protect privacy and wellbeing. Finally, we prepare you to troubleshoot common challenges—from technical glitches to interpersonal conflicts—so you can engage confidently and sustainably.

9.1 Finding Your Community

The quest to find an online community that truly resonates with your interests, goals, and style is both an art and a science. Just as explorers of old mapped uncharted territories, today's digital navigators sift through an ever-growing landscape of groups, forums, and networks to discover spaces where meaningful connection, learning, and collaboration flourish. With countless options avail-

able, this pursuit requires a deliberate approach—one
that begins with introspection and proceeds through informed exploration, critical evaluation, and thoughtful
engagement.

- **Clarify Your Interests**

  Before embarking on a search, it pays to clearly
  define what drives you. Pinpointing your
  passions, skills, and objectives sharpens your
  focus and saves precious time. Are you seeking a
  community to deepen expertise in a niche subject,
  or are you hoping for a supportive social circle to
  share hobbies? Maybe your goal is mentorship,
  project collaboration, or just casual exchange.
  Understanding these motives—whether they
  are learning a new language, improving coding
  abilities, or cultivating a wellness routine—guides
  your path. The clearer your compass, the more
  likely it is you'll find other travelers heading in the
  same direction.

  Reflection here can be surprisingly revealing.
  Consider jotting down specific interests and
  related keywords, alongside preferred interaction
  styles (formal vs. casual, synchronous chat vs.
  asynchronous forums). This mental groundwork
  serves as a foundation for the search strategies
  that follow.

- **Use Search Tools**

  Armed with a sharpened focus, your next step is
  to harness the power of search. Most platforms
  boast robust features tailored to surfacing groups
  by topic, popularity, or activity level. Hashtags, for
  instance, act as digital breadcrumbs leading to clusters of content and communities centered around

a shared theme. On platforms like Twitter, Instagram, or Reddit, entering these can immediately reveal vibrant conversations and groups.

Beyond built-in search bars, external aggregators and directories offer curated lists of communities. Websites that specialize in cataloging forums, chat servers, or social media groups—sorted by subject, size, or purpose—can save hours of trial and error. The ability to filter by criteria such as language, region, or membership type further refines results. Savvy seekers often combine platform-native tools with these external resources, creating a layered approach that casts a wider yet targeted net.

- **Leverage Recommendations**

  The digital world may be vast, but some of the best guidance comes from trusted people. Don't underestimate the power of asking peers, mentors, or seasoned community members for referrals. Often, a single recommendation can open the door to a thriving group that algorithms might overlook.

  Recommendations frequently carry context and nuance—details about a community's culture, typical member profile, or hidden perks—that cannot be gleaned from surface-level browsing. Online reviews, blog posts, or testimonials also enrich this picture, offering firsthand accounts of what it's really like inside. This social proof acts as a compass needle, pointing you toward trusted spaces and away from less constructive environments.

- **Compare Multiple Platforms**

  Not all communities live under the same roof, and not all roofs suit every dweller. Forums,

chat applications, social networks, and mailing
lists each harbor distinct atmospheres and
functionality. Forums often support deep,
threaded discussions ideal for in-depth analysis;
chat apps emphasize real-time interaction and
spontaneity; social networks blend multimedia
sharing with socializing; mailing lists suit
asynchronous, curated exchanges.

Evaluating which format best matches your expectations is crucial. For example, if you crave slow,
thoughtful debate, a Twitter hashtag or fast-paced
Discord channel might feel overwhelming. Conversely, if you enjoy lively conversation and quick
feedback, a slow-moving listserv could frustrate.
Sampling different platforms, ideally on subjects
you care about, builds familiarity with their unique
dynamics and helps identify your ideal home.

- **Document Your Options**

To keep track amidst the digital bustle, maintain
a shortlist of promising communities. A simple
spreadsheet or journal noting each group's name,
main focus, platform type, size, activity level, and
any initial impressions aids comparison. Highlight
pros and cons gleaned from cursory exploration or
feedback.

This habit not only organizes your thoughts but
also encourages reflection. By systematically
weighing options, you avoid impulsive commitments and instead base decisions on reasoned
evaluation. Updating your list as you gather new
insights keeps your search adaptive and focused.

- **Trial Participation**

Once you narrow down candidates, resist the
rush to dive in headfirst. Many communities

248

welcome newcomers as lurkers or guests—observers who watch interactions without active contribution. This trial period is invaluable, offering a low-pressure way to sense group dynamics, conversational tone, and overall vibe.

During this phase, pay attention to what members talk about, how questions are handled, and whether newcomers are greeted warmly or met with skepticism. Some platforms allow limited posting or subscribing before full membership; these afford safe testing grounds. Think of this as dating before a long-term commitment: take your time to assess chemistry.

- **Review Content Quality**

  The substance of discussions reveals much about a community's value. High-quality content reflects relevance, depth, and a constructive tone. Look for well-articulated posts, thoughtful responses, and a balance between expert knowledge and beginner accessibility.

  Communities dominated by repetitive, shallow, or off-topic chatter may offer limited growth or enjoyment. Conversely, groups where members challenge ideas respectfully, share useful resources, and encourage curiosity tend to foster richer engagement and learning. With careful observation, you'll discern whether a group elevates your interests or merely fills space with noise.

- **Evaluate Community Size**

  Size matters, but not always in obvious ways. Large groups promise diversity, frequent activity, and quick feedback, yet risk anonymity and

disorganization.   Smaller communities offer
intimacy, stronger bonds, and often more
accountability, though activity may ebb and
flow.

Consider also growth trends: Is the community
stable, expanding, or shrinking?   Rapid growth
signals vitality but may change culture unpredictably; decline might suggest waning interest
or unresolved conflicts. Ideally, choose a group
whose size and trajectory align with the experience
you desire—whether lively crowd or cozy enclave.

- **Assess Tone and Culture**

  The social fabric of a community—its tone
  and culture—shapes your sense of belonging
  more than policies or features.   Notice etiquette
  norms, language style, and inclusivity.   Is
  humor embraced, or seriousness expected?   Are
  disagreements handled with kindness or sparking
  flame wars?   Do members respect differences in
  background, opinion, and expertise?

  A welcoming culture encourages participation and
  growth, while a toxic atmosphere can stifle expression and breed frustration. This cultural chemistry
  often becomes apparent quickly during trial participation and browsing. Trust your instincts alongside objective observations.

- **Check Governance Style**

  Finally, explore how communities govern
  themselves.   Moderation styles vary from
  hands-off laissez-faire to strict rule enforcement.
  Strong moderation can protect members from
  harassment, spam, and misinformation, fostering
  safety and constructive discourse.   However,

overly rigid control may stifle spontaneity or exclude diverse views.

Investigate who holds authority—paid moderators, volunteer members, or democratic processes—and how they communicate rules and handle disputes. Transparent and fair governance generally correlates with healthier communities. Understanding this structure helps ensure your engagement aligns with your expectations for order and freedom.

By methodically navigating these steps—defining your interests, employing multiple search strategies, collecting recommendations, comparing platforms, maintaining clear records, and thoughtfully sampling communities—you set the stage for discovering rich and rewarding digital neighborhoods. In an age when connection can be just a click away, this deliberate search turns random scrolling into meaningful belonging, transforming the vast internet into a mosaic of places where you not only find others, but find yourself.

9.2 Introducing Yourself and Joining In

Stepping into a new online space can feel a bit like entering a bustling party where everybody already knows each other. The challenge is not only to be seen and heard but to do so in a way that feels natural and respected. This means more than just selecting a username or making a quick post; it involves thoughtfully crafting your presence from the very first moment. Establishing a positive reputation and meaningful connections hinges on a blend of observation, respect, and participation that many

seasoned community members develop intuitively—yet
which novices can learn to master with deliberate effort.

Before typing a single word, it is wise to *observe before
engaging*. Communities develop unique rhythms: some
conversations unfold rapidly like an energetic debate,
others move with a slower, more deliberate pace. By
simply watching threads or chat rooms, newcomers
begin to sense which topics inspire enthusiasm and
who the key contributors are. This apprenticeship
stage is critical because it lays the groundwork for
understanding not only what is discussed, but how it is
discussed. What tone is preferred? Is humor embraced
or frowned upon? Are posts formal or casual? This
quiet reconnaissance helps avoid missteps that might
come from jumping in too soon or inappropriately.

Equally important is to *understand platform etiquette*, a
term signifying the unwritten social contracts specific
to each online environment. For example, the norm on
one forum might encourage lengthy, detailed posts rich
in citations and footnotes, while another favors short,
conversational exchanges peppered with emojis. Many
communities cultivate their own jargon—specialized
terms or acronyms—and may use distinct conventions
for signatures, quoting, or replying. Familiarity with
these cultural markers shows respect and signals that
you are there to contribute thoughtfully, not merely to
broadcast your own thoughts.

Closely linked to etiquette is the necessity to *respect
posting guidelines*—the official rules about how content
should be formatted and categorized. These guidelines
often cover everything from appropriate language and
taboo topics to requirements for tagging posts and using
templates. They not only keep the community organized
and civil, but they also enhance discoverability and
engagement. For instance, tagging a question with

the correct category ensures knowledgeable members will see it. Ignoring these norms can lead to posts being overlooked, flagged, or even removed, potentially discouraging sincere newcomers.

To avoid such pitfalls, it pays to *use proper channels* for your contributions. Online platforms typically segment conversations by themes or activities, whether in forums, social media groups, or chat channels. Posting your inquiry about programming in a general discussion area rather than a dedicated technical thread might result in fewer helpful responses or misplaced moderation. Aligning your participation with the intended space signals consideration, helps maintain clarity, and connects you with the right audience.

Once you have absorbed this background knowledge, attention turns to *crafting your profile*, which acts as your virtual handshake and business card. A well-considered profile bio—concise yet informative—offers a glimpse into who you are, your interests, or expertise, allowing others to find common ground or assess your reliability. Selecting an avatar that reflects your personality can enhance memorability and approachability, but it should fit the community's tone to avoid unintended impressions. Highlighting relevant skills or experiences subtly positions you as a potential resource, inviting engagement on shared topics.

Managing your interactions effectively also involves *setting notification preferences* thoughtfully. The flood of alerts from every reply, mention, or new post can quickly overwhelm, leading to disengagement or missed important conversations. Striking a balance by customizing which notifications matter most—such as direct replies or messages in favored threads—enables you to stay informed without fatigue, maintaining sustained, manageable involvement.

Armed with preparation, it's time to *make a first post*—
not a mere formality but an opportunity to set a tone
and introduce yourself warmly. Many communities
provide dedicated "introductions" sections expressly
for new members; using these signals your awareness of
community structure and offers an inviting space
to share your background, motives for joining,
or expectations. A friendly, brief message fosters
receptivity and opens pathways for others to respond,
guiding you into the conversational flow.

Beyond simply announcing your presence, *asking
onboarding questions* can demonstrate engagement
and eagerness to integrate. Inquiring politely about
unspoken rules, resource recommendations, or tips
for newcomers leverages the collective knowledge
of veterans and invites mentorship. Such questions
function as icebreakers, positioning you as someone
respectful and motivated to contribute rather than
passively consume.

As support and guidance arrive, it is important to
express gratitude genuinely. Thanking those who assist
you, whether with a detailed answer, a helpful link, or
encouragement, builds goodwill and humanizes your
name. Gratitude is a social glue reinforcing positive
interaction and often encourages further collaboration
or friendship.

Finally, to *build an initial reputation*, one need not always
create original posts. Engagement by up-voting, liking,
or acknowledging others' contributions signals attentiveness and appreciation, amplifying valuable voices. Such
gestures provide subtle but clear evidence of your participation and respect for the community's collective enterprise. Over time, this involvement aggregates into a
reputation that encourages trust and openness, easing
future exchanges.

In essence, establishing yourself in an online community entails a subtle dance of listening, learning, adapting, and contributing. Each step—from observing conversations to expressing thanks—adds brushstrokes to the portrait of a positive, reliable member. Remember, your digital presence is a social construct, formed as much by how you join as by the ideas you share. Joining well is not merely about visibility but about weaving yourself organically into the ongoing story of a community.

9.3 Building Positive Relationships

Trust, reciprocity, and supportive connections form the lifeblood of any thriving community or collaboration. While the earlier sections have illuminated the importance of communication and understanding, this stage zeroes in on practical strategies to deepen bonds and nurture a network that not only grows but endures.

One of the most fundamental methods to foster trust is *active listening*. This goes beyond simply hearing words—it requires immersing oneself fully in what the other person conveys. Summarizing key points reflects attentiveness and respect; it shows that you value their perspective enough to grasp it clearly. Asking clarifying questions further confirms your engagement and helps prevent misunderstandings. Genuine interest is communicated not just through words but through tone, body language, and timely responses. For instance, in a workplace setting, when a colleague shares a challenge they're facing, a careful listener might respond, "So you're saying the deadline changes made it tough to coordinate with your team—have you considered adjusting the workflow to accommodate that?" Such exchanges affirm that you are genuinely invested in their experience, laying a foundation for mutual trust.

Sharing personal touchpoints is another invaluable approach. When you disclose relevant experiences or anecdotes, you humanize interactions and dissolve barriers. It's the subtle art of making conversation less transactional and more relatable. Consider a mentorship conversation: a mentor who shares their own early-career struggles not only demonstrates empathy but signals openness, encouraging the mentee to share candidly in return. These personal glimpses create emotional resonance, anchoring relationships with authenticity. Even in casual social groups, brief stories about one's background or interests can spark connections otherwise dormant.

A vibrant community thrives on reciprocity, the unspoken but potent norm that encourages mutual support. When someone assists you, responding with gratitude and offering help in return cements a cycle of kindness. Reciprocity might look like sharing resources, providing constructive feedback, or simply being available for advice later on. These small but meaningful exchanges accumulate into durable alliances. The history of human cooperation abounds with evidence that societies who embraced reciprocity norms outperformed those who did not, underscoring its primal significance to collective well-being. Bearing this in mind encourages us to adopt generosity not as obligation, but as a natural rhythm of give and take.

In the digital age, *private messaging* has become a double-edged sword for relationship-building. Direct messages invite intimacy and immediacy, but their misuse can quickly erode trust. Respectful etiquette dictates that you avoid unsolicited outreach or spamming—indeed, inundating someone with messages uninvited can swiftly alienate. Instead, private messages should be purposeful and considerate. For example, requesting advice should be prefaced by a polite introduction, explaining why you reached out personally. This respect for boundaries acknowledges the recipient's time and signals your sincerity, ensuring your message is welcomed rather than dismissed.

No relationship grows without moments of challenge, and how one navigates feedback is critical to maintaining goodwill. Handling criticism gracefully means receiving it openly, thanking the giver, and thoughtfully adjusting your approach when appropriate. This mindset reflects maturity and humility—qualities that build trust more effectively than defensiveness or dismissal. An environment where feedback is welcomed encourages transparency and continuous improvement, transforming potential friction into productive dialogue. For instance, if a project collaborator points out a weakness in your proposal, responding with, "Thanks for pointing that out—I hadn't considered it that way. Let me revise this and get back to you," strengthens the partnership by valuing honesty.

Consistency is the unseen thread weaving reliability into relationships. By contributing regularly—whether through sharing insights, participating in discussions, or simply checking in—you affirm your presence and commitment. This steady engagement helps others to see you as dependable and trustworthy. In organizational cultures, consistent contributors often become informal hubs of knowledge and support, subtly reinforcing their social capital. Conversely, erratic or absent participation risks obscurity and isolation. The rhythm of steady involvement, rather than occasional bursts, nurtures a climate of mutual understanding and anticipation.

Acknowledging milestones is a simple yet powerful way
to deepen connections by showing you notice and care
about others' achievements and life events. Whether it's
congratulating a colleague on a promotion, celebrating
project completions, or marking anniversaries of
collaboration, such gestures affirm the human
dimension of interactions. Recognition fosters
goodwill and encourages people to invest further
in relationships, as their contributions feel noticed
and valued. Personalized acknowledgments—like a
handwritten note or a public shout-out—carry emotive
weight that transcends mere formality.

Cultivating relationships within *subgroups* or smaller
communities amplifies connection quality. Special-
interest channels, project teams, or working groups
create intimate spaces where shared focus fosters trust
more quickly. These micro-communities enable more
meaningful exchange through common goals and
frequent interaction. Joining subgroups is not just about
expanding networks but enriching them with diverse
perspectives united by shared objectives. Such focused
engagement can accelerate learning, provide mutual
support, and surface leadership opportunities that
larger, more impersonal assemblies cannot.

Expanding beyond immediate circles to *cultivate
diverse ties* enhances both resilience and creativity in
relationships. Connecting across roles, geographies,
and expertise levels invites fresh viewpoints and
resourcefulness while broadening social capital.
Diversity in ties creates bridges across silos, enabling
ideas and support to flow in unexpected and enriching
directions. A cross-functional team member who
regularly interfaces with marketing, engineering, and
customer support is better positioned to anticipate
challenges and foster collaboration than one confined

to a single domain. Actively seeking such varied interactions injects vitality and adaptability into any network.

As experience grows, offering *mentorship* can be a profound way to give back and strengthen community bonds. Volunteering guidance to newcomers establishes a legacy of support and reinforces social cohesion. Mentorship not only benefits the mentee with wisdom and encouragement but also enriches the mentor through reflection and renewed purpose. This dynamic embodies a continuum of relationship-building, where knowledge and trust cascade across generations. Through mentorship, trust powers forward, creating a culture of care that perpetuates itself.

In essence, building positive relationships is both an art and a discipline—one that invites conscious effort and heartfelt engagement. By actively listening, sharing authentically, practicing reciprocity, respecting communication boundaries, embracing feedback, maintaining presence, celebrating others, engaging in focused groups, diversifying connections, and mentoring generously, we weave networks that are not just functional but deeply supportive. These strategies transform mere acquaintance into meaningful alliance, seeding communities robust enough to thrive in complexity and change.

9.4 Contributing Valuably

Engagement within any community flourishes when its members contribute in meaningful ways. Merely participating is not enough; valuable contributions—those that address real needs and enrich the collective experience—build trust, knowledge, and a sense of belonging. Learn-

ing how to add such value requires more than enthusiasm; it calls for keen observation, thoughtful communication, and a readiness to step beyond oneself. The
techniques discussed here provide a roadmap for transforming good intentions into lasting impact.

A foundational step in crafting valuable contributions is
to *identify needs*. In virtually every discussion or collaborative space, gaps exist—unanswered questions, missing resources, or opportunities to improve clarity and
functionality. Scanning conversations carefully reveals
these openings. For instance, a recurring question left
unresolved in a forum signals a point of friction, an area
where focused intervention can turn curiosity into clarity. Similarly, noticing that certain tutorials or explanations are outdated or overly complex creates a chance to
develop updated or simplified materials, directly benefiting newcomers and veterans alike. This proactive approach demands attentiveness not just to spoken queries
but also to the unsaid: what knowledge might newcomers lack, or what obstacles have yet to be illuminated?

Once a need is recognized, the ability to *ask good questions*
becomes a powerful tool, especially for those who are
still exploring. A well-crafted inquiry respects the time
and expertise of others by being clear, concise, and
context-rich. Instead of vague frustrations, an effective
question outlines what was tried, what was expected,
and where exactly confusion arises. For example, rather
than asking "How do I fix this error?", specifying
"When using version 3.2 of the software, I received
the following error message after executing command
X, despite following the documented steps. Could
someone clarify what might cause this?" invites precise,
targeted responses. This technique transforms a simple
ask into an invitation for collaborative problem-solving.

Conversely, those with deeper experience make their

mark by *providing useful answers*. Effective answers go beyond quick fixes; they guide others through the reasoning process, explain underlying principles, and offer additional resources as appropriate. Step-by-step instructions, combined with illustrative examples or analogies, demystify complex topics and empower learners to internalize solutions rather than merely copy them. For example, instead of stating "Use command Y," a valuable response might explain why command Y works in this context, potential pitfalls, and alternative approaches. This not only solves immediate problems but also cultivates independent thinking within the community.

Complementing answers, the deliberate act of *sharing resources*—whether tutorials, articles, or specialized tools—amplifies collective knowledge. Curating and recommending well-selected materials saves others time and effort, sparking deeper exploration and innovation. For instance, linking to a beginner-friendly video tutorial on a thorny concept can turn confusion into comprehension. Importantly, shared resources should be regularly reassessed to ensure their relevance and accessibility, preventing the community from becoming weighed down by outdated or overly technical materials.

Groups thrive when members *lead by example*, modeling best practices in tone, formatting, and collaboration. Clear, respectful communication fosters an inviting atmosphere that encourages participation by minimizing misunderstandings and frustration. Formatting posts with thoughtful layout— using headings, bullet points, or code blocks where applicable—enhances readability and shows care for the audience. Demonstrating openness to alternative viewpoints and constructive criticism embodies the spirit of collective growth, setting a standard that others naturally emulate. In this way, leadership is less about authority and more about creating the conditions where others feel empowered to contribute.

Beyond individual acts, creating durable contributions such as *guides and FAQs* addresses recurring questions and onboarding challenges. These evergreen documents distill accumulated wisdom into accessible references, smoothing the journey for newcomers while reducing redundant queries. Imagine the efficiency gained when a well-crafted FAQ answers eighty percent of common issues; moderators and experienced members can then invest their energies in deeper engagement rather than repetitive troubleshooting. Developing such guides requires synthesizing community feedback and iterating on clarity and completeness, often in collaboration with others to ensure inclusivity and accuracy.

Taking on more formal responsibilities by *volunteering for roles* deepens one's impact. Moderator duties, event organization, or asset maintenance exemplify commitment and service. These roles, though sometimes demanding, are crucial to sustaining community health and momentum. Moderators, for instance, not only enforce guidelines but also nurture constructive dialogue, resolve conflicts, and help new members assimilate. Event organizers curate shared experiences like workshops or contests that forge connections and spark creativity. Consistent stewardship signals investment in the community's longevity and inspires trust from peers.

Coordinating collective efforts through *projects* invites members to channel individual strengths into shared goals. Hackathons, study groups, or sprint sessions become incubators for rapid learning, troubleshooting, and solution-building that no isolated participant could achieve alone. Leadership in these contexts entails setting objectives, managing tasks, and fostering inclusive collaboration. Even joining ongoing projects contributes momentum and diversity of thought. Collaborative work not only produces tangible outputs— code, research, documentation—but also weaves social bonds that fortify community resilience.

Valuable contributors also practice *encouraging others*, recognizing efforts and motivating continued participation. Genuine praise validates the often invisible labor behind contributions and builds confidence. For example, acknowledging someone's insightful answer or new member's thoughtful question can shift their involvement from occasional to enthusiastic. Encouragement cultivates a culture where risk-taking and experimentation are welcomed, essential for innovation and growth. Even subtle gestures of appreciation—"Thanks for sharing this!" or "Great point, I hadn't considered that"—amplify positivity and reinforce collective engagement.

Finally, humility paired with curiosity is crucial in the form of *reflecting and iterating* on one's contributions. Soliciting feedback reveals unforeseen blind spots and helps align efforts with community needs. Perhaps a tutorial was too technical or a project's goals unclear; recognizing these allows for adjustments that enhance effectiveness. Reflection also guards against burnout, prompting contributors to balance ambition with sustainability. This ongoing refinement is a hallmark of mature participation—valuing quality over quantity, responsiveness over rigidity.

Taken together, these techniques form an interconnected framework for contributing meaningfully to any communal endeavor. By attentively identifying needs, communicating with clarity, sharing expertise generously, modeling constructive behavior, formalizing knowledge, assuming responsibility, promoting collaboration, uplifting peers, and evolving thoughtfully, contributors transform isolated actions into collective progress. Such engagement elevates communities from mere aggregations of individuals to dynamic networks of shared purpose and mutual growth.

9.5 Protecting Your Privacy and Wellbeing

Navigating the digital world with confidence requires more than just technical savvy—it demands a deliberate approach to preserving your privacy and mental health. As digital interactions increasingly blend with daily life, setting thoughtful boundaries becomes essential. Adjusting privacy settings, managing notifications, and cultivating mental resilience are not merely optional; they are vital tools to protect your wellbeing amid the relentless hum of online activity.

The first step in safeguarding your digital presence lies in taking control of your privacy settings. Most platforms offer a dizzying array of options to adjust who can see your profile, what information is shared, and which third-party apps may access your data. By carefully tailoring these options, you limit exposure to unwanted eyes and reduce the risk of data leakage. For example, toggling to "friends only" or "private" profiles, restricting location sharing, and scrutinizing app permissions can create a digital shield, controlling not only what you share but with whom. This proactive stance minimizes vulnerabilities and shapes your digital persona on your terms.

Equally crucial is protecting your personal data by exercising discretion about what you post. The internet never forgets, and seemingly trivial details—birthdays, pet's names, or habitual locations—can be pieced together to compromise your security or identity. Using pseudonyms or anonymized profiles in certain contexts protects your real-life identity, especially in public or semi-public forums. Beyond security, this practice offers psychological distance, allowing you to engage without constant personal exposure. Prudence in sharing builds a buffer against unintended consequences, from identity theft to digital harassment.

As connectivity grows, so does the barrage of notifications clamoring for attention. Without boundaries, the ceaseless alerts fragment focus and spike stress levels. Customizing notifications—choosing which apps can buzz, beep, or flash—helps regain control. Muting entire channels or groups during critical work or downtime fosters calm, while scheduling device-free periods cultivates mental space for reflection and relaxation. These deliberate pauses counterbalance the addictive pull of instant responses and safeguard concentration from erosion.

Complementing notification management is the mindful regulation of screen time. Extensive digital engagement can quickly spiral into burnout if left unchecked. Tools such as timers and focus modes serve as guardians, prompting regular breaks and encouraging moments to step back from the screen. These intentional intervals are not frivolous but essential acts of self-preservation; they protect eyesight, reduce cognitive fatigue, and strengthen mental clarity. Balancing productivity with rest prevents the subtle slide from healthy engagement into compulsive usage.

Maintaining a clear boundary between work and personal life further reinforces digital wellbeing. In an era when jobs often demand constant availability, defining explicit participation hours reclaims your time. Silence after hours and on weekends is not negligence but self-respect, nurturing personal relationships and individual identity beyond professional roles. When colleagues and clients understand and respect these limits, it cultivates a culture that honors human rhythms rather than 24/7 accessibility.

Yet technology's challenge is not only external but internal. Practicing mindful engagement means pausing before posting or responding, reflecting on tone, and choosing constructive language. Online communication—stripped of nonverbal cues—often breeds misunderstandings or escalates conflicts. Approaching interactions with empathy reduces digital friction and fosters healthier conversations. This habit also cultivates a sense of agency, empowering you to rise above impulsive reactions and contribute positively to digital communities.

Within these dynamics lurks the pervasive shadow of impostor syndrome—feelings of inadequacy despite evidence of competence. Online spaces, with their curated highlights and constant comparisons, can exacerbate self-doubt. Recognizing these patterns is crucial: instead of silence or retreat, adopting growth-mindset affirmations reframes challenges as opportunities to learn. Acknowledging your progress and strengths cocreates resilience against the corrosive effects of self-criticism that undermine wellbeing.

When encounters cross into harassment or abuse, digital platforms increasingly offer tools to intervene personally and collectively. Using block, mute, and report functions swiftly cuts off toxic interactions and signals community standards. These mechanisms shift some power back to users, reducing the emotional toll of negativity. Relying on these features is an act of self-defense, and in communities with active moderation, it also contributes to safer environments for all.

No one should feel isolated in managing these challenges. Seeking support—from moderators who enforce rules, mentors who provide guidance, or mental-health resources—strengthens your digital resilience. Many platforms now integrate access to counseling or peer-support networks, reflecting growing recognition that digital wellbeing is vital. Reaching out is not a sign of weakness but wisdom, acknowledging that interconnectedness implies mutual care.

Lastly, digital wellbeing flourishes through balanced self-care routines that extend beyond the screen. Engaging in offline activities—exercise, hobbies, nature walks—restores mental equilibrium and creativity. These habits replenish emotional reserves depleted by virtual demands and ground you in the tangible world. Consistent self-care is a foundation upon which all digital boundaries and protections rest; it sustains the energy and clarity to navigate digital life with intention rather than reaction.

Protecting your privacy and wellbeing in an increasingly digital world is an ongoing, active process. It requires awareness, discipline, and kindness toward oneself and others. By mastering the art of setting boundaries—whether through settings, time management, or mindful communication—you cultivate a digital existence that supports, rather than undermines, your overall health and happiness.

9.6 Troubleshooting Challenges

Navigating collaborative environments—be they digital communities, project teams, or creative

endeavors—inevitably involves encountering obstacles
that test patience, communication, and resilience.
Troubleshooting these challenges is less about avoiding
problems entirely and more about how we prepare for
and respond to them. This section explores common
yet often underestimated issues such as technical
glitches, miscommunication, motivational dips, and
interpersonal conflicts, offering practical strategies to
maintain a positive and productive atmosphere.

Overcoming Technical Issues

No matter how polished a platform or tool may seem,
technical issues are a near-constant companion in
any digital or hybrid workspace. When bugs arise,
they tend to disrupt workflows and cause frustration
that can ripple through a community. Tackling these
glitches effectively means more than just a quick
fix. It begins with reporting problems clearly and
contextually: describe not just what went wrong, but
under what circumstances it happened—what you
were doing, which device or version you used, and
any error messages encountered. This contextual detail
turns a vague complaint into actionable intelligence for
developers or support teams.

Equally important is seeking peer workarounds. Within
communities, users often share tips and temporary fixes
faster than official channels can respond. Engaging
with these informal networks not only accelerates
resolution but also fosters a helpful, communal spirit.
Meanwhile, keeping software and tools updated
remains foundational. Updates frequently patch known
vulnerabilities and improve stability; neglecting this
basic maintenance is akin to ignoring routine health
checkups—it invites problems.

Handling Miscommunication

Even seasoned collaborators stumble when communication falters. Misunderstandings creep in whenever intentions are unclear or assumptions run wild. The antidote lies in clarity and curiosity. Instead of leaping to hasty conclusions, pause and ask follow-up questions that illuminate the speaker's true meaning. Simple queries like "Could you elaborate on that?" or "What do you mean by this part?" invite clarification and signal respect for the other's perspective.

Avoiding assumptions is crucial because what seems obvious to one person may be opaque to another. This attentiveness prevents minor confusions from snowballing into larger conflicts. Language is inherently imprecise, and tone is notoriously difficult to convey in text; thus, erring on the side of explicitness, especially when discussing sensitive issues, pays dividends in maintaining harmony.

Resolving Conflict

When conflicts arise, emotions often run high, obscuring rational dialogue. Effective resolution depends on structured mediation steps that re-center the conversation around understanding rather than confrontation. Active listening is the first pillar: give the other party your full attention, reflecting back what you hear to confirm accuracy without judgment. This alone diffuses tension by demonstrating you value their perspective.

Using neutral, non-accusatory language helps prevent escalation. Instead of "You did this wrong," framing concerns as "I felt confused when..." opens space for empathy. If a dispute intensifies, shifting the discussion to private channels avoids public spectacles and preserves dignity on both sides. Through these methods, conflict can become an opportunity for growth rather than division.

Dealing with Trolling

Trolling—the deliberate provocation to elicit emotional responses or disrupt conversations—presents a unique challenge in online settings. The most important strategy is to recognize baiting tactics without feeding them. Responding emotionally often plays into a troll's hands, perpetuating negativity.

Instead, rely on moderation tools thoughtfully: muting, blocking, or reporting disruptive behavior helps preserve group health without descending into personal retaliation. Community guidelines that clearly define unacceptable conduct empower participants to collectively uphold standards. A shared understanding of boundaries ensures that trolls remain the exception, not the norm.

Adapting to Policy Changes

Platforms and communities evolve, sometimes implementing new rules or altering existing ones. Such policy changes can jar users, especially if introduced abruptly or without clear explanation. Staying informed means actively reviewing updated guidelines and reflecting on how your behavior aligns with them.

Adaptation is less about begrudging compliance and more about recognizing when changes serve collective interests—whether protecting privacy, enhancing fairness, or improving security. Proactively adjusting one's conduct avoids inadvertent violations and signals respect for the community's evolving norms, thereby fostering trust and continuity.

Escalating When Necessary

Not every problem can be resolved through peer conversations or self-help. Knowing when to escalate issues—to moderators, administrators, or platform support—is a vital skill. Such escalation should follow measured attempts at resolution, ensuring that the concern is legitimate and well-documented.

When approaching these authorities, provide concise accounts of the issue, efforts made to resolve it, and the impact on the community. This clarity expedites appropriate intervention and prevents trivial complaints from overwhelming support systems. Escalation is not a sign of failure, but rather an acknowledgment that some challenges require collective oversight and expertise.

Rebuilding Trust

Mistakes happen; they are an intrinsic part of human interaction. What follows errors often matters more than the errors themselves. Rebuilding trust after misunderstandings or missteps demands sincerity: a straightforward apology that acknowledges harm without excuses can disarm resentment.

Making amends—by correcting misinformation, clarifying intentions, or offering restitution—demonstrates commitment to the relationship. Trust solidifies over time through consistent, reliable behavior. This process transforms temporary ruptures into deeper foundations for future cooperation.

Reigniting Motivation

Sustaining engagement is perhaps the most subtle challenge of all. Enthusiasm ebbs and flows, and periods of low motivation risk disengagement. To rekindle momentum, set small, attainable goals that provide frequent opportunities for accomplishment and positive feedback.

Revisiting highlights—successful projects, celebrated community moments, or inspiring testimonials—

reminds participants why they joined in the first place. Celebrating progress, no matter how incremental, builds a culture of encouragement that buffers against burnout and disillusionment.

Planning for Downtime

Technological platforms occasionally undergo maintenance or experience outages, disrupting routine access and participation. Anticipating such downtime by preparing alternatives—such as offline activities, backup communication channels, or asynchronous tasks—minimizes disruption.

This forward-thinking approach fosters resilience; communities that can pivot gracefully during interruptions maintain cohesion and avoid frustration. Sharing clear notices about anticipated downtimes or unplanned outages promotes transparency and collective patience.

Exiting Gracefully

In any long-term endeavor, individuals will eventually move on. Whether stepping down from a role, leaving a project, or exiting a community, departing with consideration leaves doors open for future collaborations. Providing advance notice, coupled with clear summaries of ongoing work and responsibilities, ensures a smooth transition for those who stay behind.

Such exit rituals underscore respect for shared efforts and acknowledge that community is built not merely on individual contributions, but on continuity and mutual support.

Together, these troubleshooting strategies form a toolkit for sustaining positive engagement amid the inevitable challenges of collaborative life. By anticipating problems, communicating openly, and responding thoughtfully, individuals and groups maintain the productive spirit that fuels innovation and shared success.